NATURE AND SUPERNATURE

ST. MICHAEL'S LECTURES, 1973
GONZAGA UNIVERSITY, SPOKANE

NATURE
AND SUPERNATURE

E. L. MASCALL

Darton, Longman & Todd
London

First published in Great Britain in 1976 by
Darton, Longman & Todd
85 Gloucester Road, London SW7 4SU

© E. L. Mascall, 1976

ISBN 0 232 51331 7

Printed in Great Britain by
Richard Clay (The Chaucer Press), Ltd.,
Bungay, Suffolk

CONTENTS

ST. MICHAEL'S LECTURES

(A Note from the Introduction by the Rector of St. Michael's Institute, Gonzaga University to the inaugural lectures of 1972)

In the fall of 1972, St. Michael's Jesuit School of Philosophy and Letters at Gonzaga University inaugurated the St. Michael's Lectures as a forum for outstanding international scholars to examine the question of God in modern thought. The theme for the lecture series is much the same as that of the famous Gifford Lectures, but the approach is not only philosophical but also theological.

The uniqueness lies primarily in the dynamic inherent in the structure of the series. A lecture in a tripartite form (over a three-day period) is given each fall. As the series unfolds, each lecturer is to enter into dialogue with the immediately preceding lecturer and, to the extent that he wishes, he may respond to other former lecturers in the series. At the same time, each expands the discussion by his or her own creative contribution. As a result there will develop an ongoing exchange among thinkers of international reputation.

BERNARD LONERGAN ON PHILOSOPHY AND THEOLOGY

In the lectures with which he inaugurated this series Fr. Bernard Lonergan took as his subject the Relationship between Philosophy of God and the Functional Specialty, Systematics, that is to say, in more conventional language and broadly speaking, the relationship between natural theology, which is a part of philosophy, and theology in the strict sense, which is concerned with the revealed truths of the Christian religion. I have said 'broadly speaking', since for Fr. Lonergan neither of these disciplines is to be conceived in the way that has become traditional in Catholic thinking. And one of the consequences of his approach, indeed the main conclusion of his discussion, is that the two disciplines should be seen as much more closely connected than has been generally the case. This is a welcome result for an Anglican like myself, for whom, to take one example, the common text-book distinction between *De Deo uno* as the subject of natural or philosophical theology and *De Deo trino* as the subject of theology in the strict sense has always seemed, while standing for an important principle, to be artificial and stylized if it is applied too drastically and inflexibly.

In the space at my disposal I cannot attempt to give a detailed critical discussion of Fr. Lonergan's thesis or of the technique upon which it is based and which he has expounded at length in his great works *Insight* and *Method in Theology*, especially the latter. Nor shall I attempt to settle the basic question which the latter work provokes about itself, namely whether Lonergan's method stands above all philosophical and theological systems as their judge or whether it stands beside them as one method among others, itself under judgment and needing justification. That is to say, is it the ultimate metamethodology, bearing its own credentials or not? In Fr. Lonergan's view it quite clearly is.

Fr. Joseph Donceel, in a kind but critical review of my book *The Openness of Being*[1] in *The Irish Theological Quarterly*[2] has taken me to task for asserting that the Transcendental Thomists who derive from Fr. Joseph Maréchal and among whom Fr. Lonergan must be numbered, feel bound to justify the validity of knowledge before they allow themselves the luxury of knowing. I accept this correction and, so far as Fr. Lonergan himself is involved, he can be quoted explicitly against this position. Thus he has himself said: 'Critically grounding knowledge isn't finding the ground for knowledge. It's already there. Being critical means eliminating the ordinary nonsense, the systematically misleading images and so on.'[3] Nevertheless, he has for some time been engaged in a friendly private war with Fr. Emerich Coreth on the question whether cognitional theory or

[1] Darton, Longman & Todd, and Philadelphia: The Westminster Press, 1971.

[2] 29 (1972), 195.

[3] Philip McShane, 'An Interview with Fr. Bernard Lonergan, S.J.', *Clergy Review*, 56 (1971), 430.

metaphysics is the primary philosophical discipline,[4] and he said quite explicitly in his lectures last year:

> The basic discipline, I believe, is not metaphysics but cognitional theory. By cognitional theory is meant, not a faculty psychology that presupposes a metaphysics, but an intentionality analysis that presupposes the data of consciousness. From the cognitional theory there can be derived an epistemology, and from both the cognitional theory and the epistemology there can be derived a metaphysics.[5]

And in many places he tells us that these three basic disciplines, cognitional theory, epistemology, and metaphysics, are respectively concerned with 'the three basic questions: What am I doing when I am knowing? Why is doing that knowing? What do I know when I do it?'[6] (We may note in passing that in *Insight* only the first and third of these questions are posed: What is happening when we are knowing? What is known when that is happening?; and the two parts of the work deal with these successively.) Personally, while I am full of admiration for Fr. Lonergan's emphasis upon the fundamentally spiritual and (in the technical sense) intentional character of our perception of the world and for his brilliant analysis of its various forms in relation to the various differentiations of consciousness, I have misgivings about taking cognitional theory as a starting-point. This may, however, mean nothing more than that there are more

[4] Cf. E. Coreth, 'Immediacy and the Mediation of Being: An Attempt to Answer Bernard Lonergan', Philip McShane, ed., *Language Truth and Meaning*, pp. 33–48.

[5] *Philosophy of God, and Theology: The Relationship between Philosophy of God and the Functional Specialty, Systematics* (London: Darton, Longman & Todd, 1973), p. 33.

[6] *Method in Theology* (London: Darton, Longman & Todd, and New York: Herder and Herder, 1972), p. 83.

ways than one of building up a philosophical system, though I suspect that Fr. Lonergan himself would repudiate any method that did not conform to his metamethodology; like the monk who put on his cowl by spreading it out on the floor and crawling into it on all fours, I am not saying that my way is the only way or even the best way; I am only saying that it is a possible way and is the way I myself do it.

With Fr. Lonergan's four precepts 'Be attentive', 'Be intelligent', 'Be reasonable', 'Be responsible', I am in full agreement. (Again, we might note in passing that the last of these, which holds a key position in *Method in Theology*, hardly appears at all in the earlier work *Insight*.) They are correlated respectively with the four acts of experience, understanding, reflection, and decision. I do not think that commentators have sufficiently remarked that these are a refinement and elaboration of the fundamental structural operations of the human soul as it is conceived in Thomist Aristotelianism. Experience corresponds to sensation; understanding and reflection to the intellectual operations of conception and judgment respectively; and all three are forms of cognition. In contrast, decision is an operation of appetition or volition. That there is this correspondence is not surprising, for Fr. Lonergan is a Transcendental Thomist, and Transcendental Thomists, whatever the traditional Thomists may say, at any rate believe themselves to be Thomists. The correspondence is, however, not altogether exact and there is a good deal of overlapping and interpenetration, which is fully accounted for by the repudiation of Aristotelian systematics which Fr. Lonergan proclaims. In spite of this, his exposition of his methodology closely follows this fourfold scheme, though, since like the famous Duke of York he first climbs up to the top of the hill and then climbs down again, its ultimate shape is not fourfold but eightfold. First the four precepts are successively manifested in 'mediating theology', in the four disciplines of Research, Interpretation, History, and Dialectic; then the reverse process of 'mediated theology' is manifested in the four disciplines of Foundations, Doctrines, Systematics, and Communications. On this eightfold path a crucial part is played by the three conversions, an intellectual conversion, which takes place between Interpretation and History in the transition from conceptualization to judgment, and moral and religious conversions, which are involved on the higher levels of History, Dialectic, and Foundations, and specially at the peak where mediating theology passes over to mediated theology. (Needless to say, here as in mystical theology, it is a matter of convention whether one uses the image of ascent followed by descent or the converse image of descent followed by ascent.) Such a very schematic account as this may well fail to do justice to the avowedly dynamic character of Fr. Lonergan's thought; it may even be suggested that he fails to do justice to it himself. The eight Functional Specialties, to use the name which he himself has given them, are certainly not to be conceived as having no horizontal interconnections, as if each was related only to its immediate predecessor and successor in the series; though any particular piece of theologizing may chiefly exemplify some particular one of them, they are no more to be thought of as mutually exclusive than are the different operations of the human soul which they manifest. Nevertheless, to distinguish is not to separate,[7] but it is rather to acquire an accurate notion of the interrelations of the factors involved; and Fr. Lonergan's classification might do much, if it was taken seriously, to bring some degree of order into the extraordinary jumble of

[7] 'Separation is one thing, distinction is another' (*Method in Theology*, p. 339).

activities which goes under the omnibus name of 'theology' in most university faculties today.

I fully appreciate Fr. Lonergan's emphasis upon the dynamic character which should belong to theology and in particular to Systematics. Doctrinal development should certainly not be envisaged on the model of Aristotelian deductive logic, as the deduction from clearly formulated premises of conclusions implicit in them but not hitherto discerned. I am not, however, altogether satisfied with the alternative which he offers. After a highly penetrating account of the way in which the systems of modern science have superseded those of medieval Aristotelianism, he expounds the third type which he himself commends, the transcendental type based on intentionality analysis. 'It differs,' he says,

> from Aristotelian system in as much as its basic terms and relations are not metaphysical but cognitional. It resembles modern science in as much as its basic terms and relations are not given to sense, but differs from modern science in as much as its basic terms and relations are given to consciousness. Unlike Aristotle and like modern science, its basic truths are not necessities but verified possibilities. Like modern science, its positions can be revised in the sense that they can be refined and filled out indefinitely; but unlike modern science, its basic structures are not open to radical revision, for they contain the conditions of any possible revision and, unless those conditions are fulfilled, revision cannot occur.[8]

In view of such passages as this, it would clearly be grossly unfair to accuse Fr. Lonergan of capitulating to the contemporary pressures for a secularized theology, a theology which takes as fundamental and unchallengeable principles the assumptions of a civilization dominated by applied science and technology. While

[8] *Philosophy of God, and Theology*, p. 8.

holding that there can be no retreat from the post-scientific to the pre-scientific differentiation of consciousness, he appeals for a movement into religious differentiation of consciousness, a differentiation which he places in God's gift of his grace. 'The exercise of the gift,' he says, 'consists in acts of love, but the gift itself is a dynamic state that fulfils the basic thrust of the human spirit to self-transcendence.'[9] 'This being in love,' he adds, 'does not presuppose or depend on any apprehension of God. It is God's free gift. He gives it not because we have sought and found him but to lead us on to seeking and finding him.'[10] To the objection *Nihil amatum nisi praecognitum*, nothing can be loved unless it is already known, he writes:

> The major exception to the Latin tag is God's gift of his love flooding our hearts. Then we are in the dynamic state of being in love. But who it is we love is neither given nor as yet understood. . . .
>
> On this showing not only is the ancient problem of the salvation of non-Christians greatly reduced, but also the true nature of Christian apologetic is clarified. The apologist's task is neither to produce in others nor to justify for them God's gift to his love. Only God can give that gift, and the gift itself is self-justifying. . . . The apologist's task is to aid others in integrating God's gift with the rest of their living.[11]

Fr. Lonergan is none the less clear about the uniqueness and plenitude of Christianity:

> If I have concluded that there is a common element to all the religions of mankind, I must now add that there is a specific element proper to Christianity. Christianity involves not only the inward gift of being

[9] *Ibid.*, p. 9.
[10] *Ibid.*, p. 10.
[11] *Method in Theology*, pp. 122–3.

in love with God but also the outward expression of God's love in Christ Jesus dying and rising again. In the paschal mystery the love that is given inwardly is focussed and inflamed, and that focussing unites Christians not only with Christ but also with one another.[12]

And, referring to his earlier work *Insight*, Fr. Lonergan modestly confesses:

I can see that the main incongruity was that, while my cognitional theory was based on a long and methodical appeal to experience, in contrast my account of God's existence and attributes made no appeal to religious experience.[13]

When he passes from Philosophy of God to Systematics, Fr. Lonergan remarks:

Modern scholarship set up an endless array of specialists between the dogmatic theologian and his sources. With the specialists the dogmatic theologian just could not compete. Without an appeal to his sources the dogmatic theologian had nothing to say. Such has been a basic and, as well, a most palpable element in the crisis of contemporary Roman Catholic theology. . . .

It is only on the basis of a full understanding and a complete acceptance of the developments in the contemporary notions of science, philosophy, and scholarship, that my account of the functional specialty, systematics, can be understood, let alone accepted. Similarly, it is only on the basis of a full acceptance of the developments in contemporary notions of science, philosophy, and scholarship that there can be understood, let alone accepted, my proposal that philosophy of God be taught by theologians in a department of theology.

My aim, of course, is not to disqualify philosophers from teaching

[12] *Philosophy of God, and Theology*, p. 10.
[13] *Ibid.*, p. 12.

or speaking about God. My aim is to qualify theologians for a task that once was theirs, and once more I believe should become theirs.[14]

In Fr. Lonergan's view, the way forward lies, as we would expect, in taking cognitional theory and not metaphysics as the basic theory.

> Instead of speaking of material objects one speaks of data, and instead of speaking of formal objects one simply applies to the data the operations prescribed by the method. While theology used to be defined as the science about God, today I believe it is to be defined as reflection on the significance of a religion in a culture. From this view of theology it follows that theology is not some one system valid for all times and places, as the Aristotelian and Thomist notion of system assumes, but as manifold as are the many cultures within which a religion has significance and value.[15]

At first sight, this might seem to be an alarming statement and to suggest the kind of complete relativism about truth and Christian doctrine that is, for example, characteristic of Dr. Leslie Dewart's books *The Foundations of Belief* and *The Future of Belief*. In fact it is nothing of the sort. What Fr. Lonergan is presupposing as unquestioned is the permanent validity of his method of intentional analysis and it is his contention that its application will result in a progressively deeper, and in principle a never-finished, understanding of the Christian mystery:

> I advocate the unity of the functional specialty, systematics, and of the philosophy of God, not on any and every set of assumptions, but only on one precise meaning of unity and only on certain assumptions concerning the meaning of objectivity, the content of the basic disciplines, the relationship between the basic and other disciplines, the nature of

[14] *Ibid.*, pp. 32–3.
[15] *Ibid.*, pp. 33–4.

system, and the concept of theology. It is on these assumptions that I shall proceed to argue that the philosophy of God and the functional specialty, systematics, have a common origin, that each complements and reinforces the other, and that they have a common goal even though they proceed in different manners.[16]

At this point it is essential to remind ourselves that for Fr. Lonergan the method is altogether different from some purely abstract and stylized system which in principle could be fed into a computer and produce conclusions in the shape of propositions by an unconscious automatic process. On the contrary, it is the exercise by the human mind of its virtually unrestricted desire to know, a desire which is radically motivated by love. Fr. Lonergan remarks:

Method can be thought of as a set of recipes that can be observed by a blockhead yet lead infallibly to astounding discoveries. Such a notion of method I consider sheer illusion. The function of method is to spell out for each discipline the implication of the transcendental precepts, Be attentive, Be intelligent, Be reasonable, Be responsible. Nor does the explicitness of method make the occurrence of discoveries infallible. The most it can achieve is to make discoveries more probable.[17]

Again he writes:

I have been contrasting a static and a dynamic viewpoint and I have been bringing the two together in a higher unity by urging that logic brings to each successive discovery the clarity, coherence, and rigour that will reveal the inadequacy of the discovery, while method shows the way from one discovery to the next. . . .

For the man that knows his logic and does not think of method,

[16] *Ibid.*, p. 50.
[17] *Ibid.*, p. 48.

objectivity is apt to be conceived as the fruit of immediate experience, of self-evident and necessary truths, and of rigorous inferences. When method is added to the picture, one may succeed in discovering that objectivity is the fruit of authentic subjectivity, of being attentive, intelligent, reasonable and responsible.[18]

This seems to me to be of vast importance. On the fundamental issue it lines up transcendental Thomists such as Bernard Lonergan and Karl Rahner with traditional Thomists such as Jacques Maritain and Etienne Gilson against the all-too-common type of philosophy which conceives perception on the analogy of the mechanical impact of elastic bodies and intellectual activity on the analogy of the functioning of an electronic computer. The theological parallel to this type of philosophy is the attitude which would have as its ideal the programming of a computer with the rules of Aristotelian logic, the feeding into it of all the contents of Denziger's *Enchiridion*, and the subsequent production of all the hitherto unformulated propositions which could be derived by the former from the latter. (This still leaves unresolved the knotty problem of the sources and compilation of Denziger!) There is no less firmly rejected another philosophical attitude which considers the objects of perception to be wholly interior to the perceiving mind, so that the existence of an external world can be known, if at all, only by inference from the contents of the mind. We have seen that for Fr. Lonergan cognitional theory should precede epistemology, and epistemology should precede metaphysics; he is nevertheless emphatic that the human mind finds itself from the start in a world whose horizon is unlimited. 'Critically grounding knowledge isn't finding the ground for knowledge. It's already there.' The title of his earlier work *Insight*

18 *Ibid.*, pp. 48–9.

indicates Fr. Lonergan's fundamental thesis: it is that knowing always consists in penetrating beneath the immediately apprehended surface of an object into its intelligible *being*. Insight is *in*sight, seeing into. In his still earlier work, *Verbum: Word and Idea in Aquinas*,[19] he generally uses the word 'understanding', which, like the Latin words *intelligentia* and *intellectus*, carries the same suggestion: 'standing under', *intus legere*, 'reading within'— a very different notion, we must remark, from 'reading into'! Thus, the human intellect has a radically dynamic character, an unlimited desire to *know*. This is at least one of Fr. Lonergan's reasons for his use of the word 'transcendence'. 'The immanent source of transcendence in man,' he writes, 'is his detached, disinterested, unrestricted desire to know,' and he sees the fact that 'man's unrestricted desire to know is mated to a limited capacity to attain knowledge'[20] as providing the basis for an argument for the existence of God.

Now if we had nothing later than the work *Insight* to refer to, Fr. Lonergan might seem to lay himself open to the accusation which has often been levelled against the traditional Thomists, that of a purely intellectualist attitude to religion; God would seem to be sought simply in order to satisfy man's restless desire to *know*. The later writing, however, has given a greater and greater place to love—both God's love for man and man's love for God; and indeed it is precisely on this ground that Fr. Lonergan argues for the unification of philosophy of God and systematics. 'Our first point,' he affirmed in his third lecture last year, 'has been that philosophy of God and the functional specialty,

[19] First published in book form, London: Darton, Longman & Todd, and Notre Dame: University of Notre Dame Press, 1967.

[20] *Insight* (London: Longmans Green and Co., and New York: Philosophical Library, 1957), pp. 636, 639.

systematics, have the same source and origin in God's gift of his love.'[21] And he makes it plan that the questioning which, like Fr. Coreth,[22] he sees as the necessary philosophical starting-point, is something more than mere curiosity. In his words:

> As I suggested in *Method in Theology*, the basic form of the question of God arises when one questions one's questioning. Now our questioning is of different kinds. There are our questions for intelligence and by them we ask what, and why, and how, and what for. There are our questions for reflection and by them we ask is that so or is it not so, is it certain or is it only probable. There are our questions for deliberation and by them we ask whether what we are doing is really worth while, whether it is truly good or only apparently good. Finally, there is the religious question: we are suffering from an unconditioned, unrestricted love; with whom, then, are we in love?[23]

And Fr. Lonergan went on to assert that, although 'the question of God arises on four different levels, it does not follow that there are four distinct and separate questions. The questions are distinct but they also are cumulative.'[24] (Without attempting a forced and unnecessary concordism, we might remember that Maritain in *The Degrees of Knowledge* found it necessary to pass from the Degrees of Rational Knowledge, in which his mentor was St. Thomas Aquinas and the guiding principle that of reason, to the Degrees of Suprarational Knowledge, in which his mentor was St. John of the Cross and the guiding principles those of love and of grace.) Fr. Lonergan admitted that 'it can quite plausibly be argued that the fourth question (the religious question) would not occur if man existed in the state of pure nature. 'In

[21] *Philosophy of God, and Theology*, pp. 52-3.

[22] *Metaphysics*, trans. Joseph Donceel (New York: Herder and Herder, 1968), p. 46.

[23] *Philosophy of God, and Theology*, pp. 52-3.

[24] *Ibid.*, p. 54.

that case,' he continued, 'the philosophy of God would not only be distinct from the functional specialty, systematics, but that functional specialty would not exist.'[25] 'But,' he pointed out, 'man at present does not exist in the hypothetical state of affairs named pure nature'; and 'it is only in the climate of religious experience that philosophy of God flourishes.'[26] Clearly, then, he sees religious conversion as important for the philosopher as well as for the theologian, and he sees the marriage of philosophy of God and systematics as advantageous for both parties; and, when he says that both disciplines have a common origin in religious experience, I am sure that he does not mean that for either discipline religious experience should be merely the object of a detached and superficial examination. That would be to reduce the philosophy of God to a mere branch of anthropology or of psychology or even of linguistics. If, however, we remember that for Fr. Lonergan, advance in understanding takes place, not by the construction of new syllogisms or the development of new techniques of computation but by what he describes as new differentiations of consciousness the state of affairs will be very different. When he writes that 'it is only in the climate of religious experience that philosophy of God flourishes', he admits, indeed he asserts, that he does not think it difficult to establish God's existence, but he sees this as only the first step in the philosophy of God. And it is only in the climate of reflection on religion that, in his view, philosophy of God acquires its full significance and attains its proper effectiveness.[27]

Thus, to bring the various strands of his thought together, for

[25] *Ibid.*, p. 55.
[26] *Ibid.*
[27] *Ibid.*, pp. 55–6.

Fr. Lonergan the human understanding, in its essential dynamism, having undergone intellectual, moral, and religious conversion, and achieving fresh differentiations of consciousness as it accepts and responds to the love of God, can arrive at a state in which philosophy of God and the functional specialty, systematics, while retaining their several identities, operate together in a fruitful and happy union which is mutually profitable and fulfilling. Thus, he maintains, theology may overcome the isolation from which it has suffered in the modern world and may once again find itself at home in the affairs of man. 'The Thomist and especially the Neothomist conceptions of philosophy and theology,' he writes, 'rest on the religious, the linguistic, the literary, and the systematic differentiations of consciousness. Commonly they are unfamiliar with the differentiations resulting from modern science, modern scholarship, and contemporary intentionality analysis.'[28]

Fr. Lonergan's final consideration is connected with the contemporary notion of person. He stresses that this comes out of genetic biology and psychology, for which the 'I' of the child emerges from the 'we' of the family, so that the primordial fact is not the person but the community. 'The person is the resultant of the relationships he has had with others and of the capacities that have developed in him to relate to others.'[29] He contrasts this with the traditional view which was 'the product of trinitarian and Christological problems as these were conceived within the systematic differentiation of consciousness as originated by Aristotle and transposed to Christian soil by Thomas Aquinas'.[30] And he asserts that the new notion of person

[28] *Ibid.*, p. 57.
[29] *Ibid.*, p. 59.
[30] *Ibid.*, p. 58.

finds fresh relevance in his view of philosophy of God and of
systematics:

> For the strongest and the best of the relationships between persons is
> love. Religious experience at its first root is the love of God with one's
> whole heart and whole soul, with all one's mind and all one's strength,
> and from it flows the love of one's neighbour as oneself. . . .
>
> It follows that, as philosophy of God and the functional specialty,
> systematics, have a common origin in religious experience, so also
> they have a common goal in the development of persons. But each
> person is one, a whole, and not just a set of parts. It follows that the
> study of what makes persons persons is not to be carried on under
> different principles and in different departments. Philosophy of God
> and the functional specialty, systematics, may and should unite.[31]

Clearly, I cannot in the space at my disposal attempt to give a
systematic critique of Fr. Lonergan's lectures, even if I felt com-
petent to do so; there are many scholars on both sides of the
Atlantic who are engaged in this task. Whether one goes all the
way with him or not, there can be no doubt whatever that he is
one of the greatest living Christian thinkers. However, before I
indicate the way in which I propose to take his exposition as a
spring-board for my two remaining lectures, I will venture to
make two comments of a critical, though I hope not hostile,
kind.

First, I am not convinced that Fr. Lonergan has sufficiently
protected the primacy of the Christian revelation over the
speculations of the human reason. It would, of course, be ridiculous
to describe him as a theological radical and to class him with
such writers as Harvey Cox, Paul van Buren, or Schubert M.
Ogden, or even with Piet Schoonenberg or Hans Küng. He has
in fact described himself as 'a Roman Catholic with quite con-

[31] *Ibid.*, p. 59.

servative views on religious and Church doctrines'[32] and he has devoted a large part of his chapter on 'Doctrines' in *Method in Theology* to demonstrating the compatibility of his views with the Vatican Council of 1870. 'I have,' he writes, 'done so deliberately, and my purpose has been ecumenical. I desire it to be as simple as possible for theologians of different allegiance to adapt my method to their uses.'[33] And he ends the book with this admirable paragraph, which combines charity and loyalty to truth most impressively:

> While the existence of division and the slowness in recovering unity are deeply to be lamented, it is not to be forgotten that division resides mainly in the cognitive meaning of the Christian message. The constitutive meaning and the effective meaning are matters on which most Christians very largely agree. Such agreement, however, needs expression and, while we await common cognitive agreement, the possible expression is collaboration in fulfilling the redemptive and constructive roles of the Christian church in human society.[34]

What worries me, however, has nothing to do with ecumenics. It is the question whether, in expressing his regret at the Church's failure to enter upon the post-medieval differentiation of consciousness and his concern that it should enter upon it now, Fr. Lonergan is giving sufficient weight to the Church's and the theologian's duty not merely to adapt theology to new patterns and contexts of thought and life but also, and primarily, to adjudicate upon the latter and, where they are in error, to correct them. Granted that the medieval synthesis was in many ways incomplete and incoherent, and even that in its own day the scholastic differentiation of consciousness was inadequate to the situation,

[32] *Method in Theology*, p. 332.
[33] *Ibid.*, pp. 332–3.
[34] *Ibid.*, p. 368.

can we be confident that post-medieval differentiation, developing as it did in less and less conscious rapport with Christian tradition, is adequate to the situation of the modern world? To take one of Fr. Lonergan's own examples, has the modern view of the person, coming out of genetic biology and psychology (to which I would add sociology and political theory) such an obvious validity that it can, without drastic revision, enter into happy union with the Christian belief about man, even if we grant that that belief was formulated as the product of trinitarian and Christological discussion within a differentiation of consciousness that was Aristotelian and Thomist and definitely pre-scientific? In brief, has Fr. Lonergan discovered the principle which we need in order to solve the pressing problem of the relation of the unchanging datum of revelation to the changing and developing cultural settings in which it has to be expressed? If he has, this will be a matter for gratitude and rejoicing, but I am not yet convinced that this is so.

My second critical reflection is that, in expounding the method which the contemporary theologian should follow, Fr. Lonergan seems to me, in his explicit statements—for I have no doubts about his personal religious orientation—to take insufficient account of the fact that the theologian is, or at any rate should be, operating within the great tradition of thought and life into which he was incorporated at baptism, the living tradition of the one, holy, catholic and apostolic Church. I am well aware of the problems that have been created for the theologian by the divisions within Christendom, by the ossifications, divagations, and ramifications which, in various times and places, have overtaken the tradition itself, and by the impact upon theology of other academic disciplines and the attitudes and assumptions of the modern secularized world. I dealt with this matter in outline in the inaugural lecture which I delivered in 1962 in the chair of Historical Theology in the University of London, and with some of its particular aspects and details in more recent writings. Here I can only reiterate that I see the function of theology and the theologian as the explication and the development of the Church's own tradition of thought and life. Theology is, I would therefore maintain, an essentially *ecclesial* activity. If I may repeat what I said in my inaugural lecture:

> As I see it, the task of the Christian theologian is that of theologizing within the great historical Christian tradition: *theologizandum est in fide*. Even when he feels constrained to criticize adversely the contemporary expressions of the tradition, he will be conscious that he is bringing out from the depths of the tradition its latent and hitherto unrecognized contents; he is acting as its organ and its exponent. He will also offer his own contribution for it to digest and assimilate if it can. Like the good householder he will bring out of his treasure things new and old. But he will have no other gospel than that which he has received.[35]

Now I do not suppose for one moment that Fr. Lonergan would disagree with this, but I wish that he had made it more explicit in his exposition of the religious differentiation of consciousness. He does indeed say that, while there is a common element to all the religions of mankind, there is a specific element proper to Christianity, and he describes this element in most warm and moving terms. But he fails to make plain what is, I think, implicit in his whole treatment, namely that this element is basically ecclesial, that the dynamic process which is the enterprise of theology down the ages takes place within the great tradition of the faith and life of the People of God, the Body of Christ.

To revert to more traditional terms, Fr. Lonergan's proposal

[35] *Theology and History* (London: Faith Press, Ltd., 1962), p. 17.

for the integration of Philosophy of God with the functional specialty Systematics represents his solution of the perennial problem of the relation between reason and revelation, which is itself a special case of the relation between nature and supernature, or between nature and grace. It is to this wider problem that I shall devote my two remaining lectures.

LECTURE ONE: DISCUSSION

Question 1:

You state in your lecture that: 'I am not convinced that Father Lonergan has sufficiently protected the primacy of the Christian revelation over the speculations of human reason.' Could you elaborate on this statement and indicate more specifically just what the grounds for your concern are?

Mascall:

I think that one point in which this remark of mine might be justified is in what he has to say about the allegedly empirical character of theology as he sees it: that it should be like the differentiation of consciousness which derives from empirical science. It seemed to me that the danger is that of taking empirical science—which after all is something only concerned with this world—as the guideline, or paradigm, for the discussion about the transcendental realities of the Christian religion.

To put it slightly differently, however adequate the concept of empirical science may be for the actual purposes of empirical science, they are not wide enough in their range, and a good many other aspects of experience are necessary to take in the

Christian revelation. The effect, as I see it—though I may mis-understand him there—is that Fr. Lonergan seems to be slightly oscillating between saying that the present-day theology, the trend of the future, should follow the differentiation of conscious-ness of empirical science, and then elsewhere saying that it should be developed within the differentiation of consciousness of religious experience. It seems to me to be a little different. I am not suggesting that Fr. Lonergan himself hasn't got a proper grasp of things, but I do feel an oscillation in him between wanting to get theology developed in the context of what is regarded as the 'popular' way of thinking of the modern world, and wanting to establish the primacy of the Christian revelation.

Question 2:

In your lecture you say: 'On this eightfold path a crucial part is played by the three conversions, an intellectual conversion, which takes place between Interpretation and History in the transition from conceptualization to judgment, and moral and religious conversions which are involved on the higher levels of History, Dialectic, and Foundations, specially at the peak where mediating theology passes over to mediated theology.' Would it not be more accurate to say that Lonergan presupposes all three conversions as already existing and operative in a theo-logian before he begins the Functional Specialties?

Mascall:

I think that what I said in the passage which you just quoted from my lecture was in fact what I derived from Lonergan's own way of speaking; it seems to me that is what he himself says. But I think we have to distinguish between the actual, concrete theologizing which a theologian is involved in and the kind of conceptual analysis of this theologizing which is what Fr. Lonergan is dealing with in his *Method in Theology*. And he does himself make the claim that the constituent specialties very much interrelate to one another. And he certainly would not suggest—though this would not be precluded—that anyone sets out to deal simply within the limitations of one of these specialties. In practice, of course, a number of them come into any instance of theological thinking.

Now if one is thinking of a particular theologian who actually is doing his theologizing and doing it seriously and not some spurious substitute, I think he will be, must be, a person who has undergone the three conversions. But it seems to me that when Lonergan produces his scheme with the eightfold path, he does suggest that these conversions have to come before, have to have taken place at a particular stage. I must admit that I find that what he has to say about conversion is one of the most difficult things in his discussion and I am not at all sure I understood it. I have spoken with others and they share my difficulty.

Question 3:

Do you think that Fr. Lonergan's attempt to work out a method which could be employed in a rigorous fashion by theologians is a realistic endeavour, or do you see the attempt to establish a universally valid theological method to be a bit impossible?

Mascall:

Well, if you think of anybody who is going to do a piece of theological work, I don't think he would deliberately chart his course by looking at Fr. Lonergan's *Method in Theology*. But what I do think is probably the case is that you can apply what Fr. Lonergan says to any particular piece of theologizing to see how far in fact it does actually conform to the method which he thinks all theology should conform to.

I think that it is something like a language. You can learn a language without in fact realizing that you are learning it, without starting off with a grammar, and so on. If anyone tried to theologize on the lines of Fr. Lonergan's method explicitly, it would be artificial. And Fr. Lonergan himself, I think, suggests that people in the past have not in fact understood this method of his as the only one to follow. If it were necessary to wait for the only valid method, then there would never be a real Christian theologian. It seems to me that the method is one which, if it is going to apply, makes it possible to see how far theologizing has been valid.

The point about which I am less happy is what seems to be Fr. Lonergan's conviction that his method is the only possible method for valid theology. And it is in fact for him not just a methodology which might serve like other alternatives, but is *the* method of methodology, the laying down of the main principles for all legitimate theologizing. And I don't think this is an easy thing to accept. But if one does say that this is the only one valid method which theology can follow, someone might ask, Why? Fr. Lonergan would, I suppose, say that we can see this as verified in the actual evidence from an intentional analysis of the human consciousness when it sets itself to deal with man's unrestricted desire to know. But I think that elsewhere he would probably say that when you are dealing with a very fundamental, basic principle, the only way you can justify it, is by trying to show the contradictions of the counterposition. He would say there is nothing more fundamental to appeal to, because this is in the nature of a fundamental principle. Therefore all you can do is see what happens if you deny it, and if you do, and you are led into contradictions, then you can assume that the principle is valid.

Question 4:

Would it be fair to ask, borrowing your words, if Thomas Aquinas has 'sufficiently protected the primacy of the Christian revelation over the speculations of human reason' since Thomas Aquinas borrowed his method from Aristotle?

Mascall:

I was referring to the argument that because Thomas Aquinas followed Aristotle, he was dechristianizing the Christian revelation, Aristotle himself not being a Christian. Well, it is an argument, but I think also we can say that St. Thomas didn't think this was what he was doing and did not unwittingly take Aristotle and simply force Christian revelation into the Aristotelian frame, because he did in effect quite violently modify Aristotle. For example, I could cite St. Thomas' opinion on the soul, and also his conception of God as not merely a final cause, but also the efficient cause of the world. Aristotle's God was not conscious of the world, whereas St. Thomas' God is the deliberate conscious creator of the world. And so, whether he is successful or not, it seems to me that Aquinas was very conscious of the need to modify Aristotle before he could really make him a vehicle for a Christian theologizing.

And I suppose that Fr. Lonergan would say the same kind of thing when he wants to take the differentiation of consciousness produced by modern science as the medium within which his theologizing be done. It seems to me that Fr. Lonergan is a little less critical of the modern scientific outlook than St. Thomas was of Aristotle. I think that actually Fr. Lonergan plays down the principles of philosophical method. One would like to see the extent to which he finds it necessary, in actually applying his method, to modify the outlook of the scientific culture in order for it to be a valid medium for Christian theology.

Question 5:

You indicate that you do not think that Lonergan in articulating the method which contemporary theologians should follow takes sufficient account of the fact that a theologian should be operating within the great tradition of thought and life into which he was incorporated at baptism. Lonergan, I hazard the guess, might reply: 'My *Method in Theology* is a methodological work, not a theological work. Moreoever, the thematization of authentic conversion constitutes the functional specialty Foundations, and this grounds the specialty Doctrines as well as Systematics and Communications. I have therefore in constituting my method made authentic—*i.e.* Christian—conversion central, and doctrines are selected and articulated within the horizon of authentic conversion.'

Mascall:

Once again, I think that Lonergan would say that this is what he is doing, what he hopes and claims to be doing, but I am not quite convinced that he does. I think it was Karl Rahner who said that the weakness of *Method in Theology* seemed to him to be that it was just simply a statement of the method which ought to be followed for any kind of valid thinking about any area of human experience, but there didn't seem to be anything particularly theological about it. If Lonergan wants to reply: 'My *Method in Theology* is a methodological work, not a theological work,' I think that somebody might answer him, 'Well, anyhow even if it is a methodological work and not a theological work—not an investigation of certain theological questions—even so, if you say it is method in theology, this does claim to lay down not just the general principles of method for any kind of human investigation, but the method proper to theology.' It does seem to me that he is not sufficiently explicit about the fact that theology does and should take place within the life of the Christian church.

I know his remarks about the religious differentiation of consciousness and the fact that Christian consciousness is more specific than religious consciousness in general, and so on. But to put it in a personal way, if I myself were to begin some theological inquiry, I don't think that I would start off by saying this is the method I am going to follow in line with what Lonergan says. I think I'd rather say how I arrived through my own reflection explicitating the content of the Christian revelation as in effect it has come to me in the life of the Church. Again, I think Lonergan, in spite of what he says about the differentiation of consciousness, does not seem to be describing something which is a very ecclesial activity. It is, but it does not seem to me that he himself, in this description of it there, sufficiently emphasizes this fact.

Question 6:

You express misgivings about taking cognitional theory as a starting point for philosophizing. Lonergan holds that it is essential in the present period of critical philosophy to do so, basically because for him being—with which metaphysics deals—must be defined in terms of knowing, since a man does not have any immediate intuition or vision or perception of concrete existence. Could you explain why you have misgivings about Lonergan's position on the need to begin with cognitional analysis and where you stand regarding the manner in which man knows concrete existence?

Mascall:

I think I stand with the traditional analysis in this matter, that of Gilson or Maritain. Although as you noticed I accepted the correction that Fr. Donceel made concerning remarks of mine about transcendental Thomists, I do think that unless you start off on the fact that we know reality, you have no foundation. If you start inquiring how we can know, and whether or not we know, before we allow ourselves to know anything, it seems to me that you can never get going, that you cannot get away from the position in which Kant found himself. And I think my attitude is that of a traditional Thomist like Gilson or Maritain. I also think it coincides with some transcendental Thomists like Emerich Coreth, who has been debating with Fr. Lonergan on this very point. I think it is probable, if not possible, that the different transcendental Thomists have not been exactly in agreement with one another on this particular matter. Fr. Lonergan seems quite explicit in saying that we must start with cognitional theory and that metaphysics must be built on the basis of cognitional theory. But Maréchal, if Fr. Donceel is right, didn't hold that at all. Maréchal held that if you adopt Kant's method of investigating the conditions of knowledge before you allow yourself to know anything, you get into a contradiction. In other words, Maréchal might seem to take Kant and christianize him, but in fact he is not christianizing Kant but trying to show that Kant cuts his own throat. The difference between the different transcendental Thomists is one of these points which I've been trying to explain here.

For me the primary datum which we have is the existence of extramental being. We perceive objects that are not ourselves. The transcendental Thomists all seem to want to say that it is we as perceivers who are the undeniable datum. They are not, of course, doing a Cartesian 'Cogito, ergo sum'. They are saying that what is given in my experience is my existence as the subject of experience. I would say what is given is the object of my experience.

2

NATURE AND SUPERNATURE

'NATURE AND GRACE', 'nature and supernature', 'the natural and the supernatural'—such phrases as these have become traditional in Christian theology and philosophy, and they obviously presuppose that there is something that can be usefully and intelligibly denoted by the noun 'nature' and the adjective 'natural'. And it is not in fact difficult to see what that is. We must however make it plain that this theological and philosophical use of the terms is very different from that in which they are sometimes used today, and were more frequently used in the past, to denote the world that stands over against man as the raw material for scientific observation and experiment, the 'physical world', as we sometimes call it, remembering (I hope) that 'physical' and 'natural' are etymologically equivalent, since *physis* means in Greek what *natura* means in Latin, the world of what is significantly called 'natural science'. This is the sense that has led to one of the leading British scientific periodicals being called simply *Nature* and to the placing on its title-page of the Wordsworthian motto 'To the solid ground of nature trusts the Mind that builds for aye.' In this sense, nature stands over against man as the object of man's observation and manipulation, though we may

notice that with the development of such disciplines as psychology, genetics, molecular biology, and sociology, man is
finding himself in the alarming position of becoming not only
the experimenter but also the experimented-upon, not only the
manipulator but also the manipulatee. In the theological sense,
however, 'nature' denotes not something standing over against
man or even an environment in which he finds himself, but an
aspect or a component of man himself, if not indeed man in his
entirety. *Nature* in the wider, scientific sense is made up of
individual *natures*, individual beings or kinds of being, and man is
one of these, so that 'human nature' simply means man himself
or the kind of being he is.

This being so, there might seem to be no place for the term
'supernature' at all. If 'human nature' simply means the kind of
being that man is, it presumably includes everything that enters
into his constitution and activity, everything that he has, is and
does. And indeed, in its theological usage 'nature' has not entirely lost its links with the scientific use; it has come to denote
those aspects of man which pertain to his membership of, and
his dealings with, the 'natural' world, the world in which he
lives his everyday life and which he manipulates by the means
with which science and technology have equipped him. But it
leaves open the question whether there are other aspects of man's
being than these, and if there are such they will not be denoted
by the term 'natural' in this theological sense.

'Natural', then, as applied to man, can be defined as everything in him that is concerned with what are sometimes significantly described as 'this life' and 'this world'. Here, 'this life'
means the life that begins with conception in the womb and ends
with bodily death, the life that begins shortly before the cradle
and ends shortly before the grave; and 'this world' means the

world which we perceive with our bodily senses and manipulate with our bodily organs. If, then, there are any aspects of man and his activity which are not concerned simply with 'this world', they may legitimately be termed 'supernatural'. This definition of 'natural' and 'supernatural' has considerable advantages. First, it is, broadly speaking, the definition that has been adopted or assumed in traditional Christian theology. Secondly, it does not presuppose or require any particular view about man's origin, resources, or destiny; the secularist will simply deny that the supernatural exists, the Christian will assert that it does, but both will mean the same thing by it. Thirdly, if the supernatural *is* believed to exist, no particular view will be presupposed as to what it is like or as to how it is related to the natural. There will thus be the possibility of discussion and controversy without the frustrating situation arising in which it is never quite clear whether the different disputants are using words in the same sense or not. And it is difficult not to suspect that this kind of ambiguity has been fairly common in recent arguments about 'nature' and 'the supernatural'.

Now it is not surprising that the existence of the supernatural should be denied by atheists and secularists. It is more surprising that its existence is denied, or at least that its mention is deprecated, by many persons who would claim to be Christians, since there is no doubt that Christ himself believed in the supernatural and it is very difficult to see what remains of Christianity if it is rejected. Nevertheless, the emotional appeal of Christianity can be very strong, even upon people whose hold upon Christian belief is non-existent or tenuous. Furthermore, the explicit repudiation of accepted formularies by ministers, or even by lay members, of religious bodies can carry unpleasant consequence with it. It is therefore not entirely inexplicable that elaborate

techniques have been devised by which traditional supernaturalistic formularies can be retained and even enthusiastically pro-
claimed (especially if they are set to music), while the original
meaning is replaced by a purely naturalistic one. One of the
most systematic attempts to do this is, of course, that made by
Dr. Paul van Buren in his book *The Secular Meaning of the Gospel*,
in which he reinterprets the traditional Christian statements so
skilfully that the reader has repeatedly to make an effort to remind himself that van Buren's basic conviction is that God does
not exist and that neither Jesus nor anyone else survives bodily
death. In a later work, he makes it clear that he can forgive
what he describes as 'the Jesus of the New Testament documents'
(it is not evident whether this is the actual historical Jesus of
Nazareth) for speaking of God as 'an intensely personal figure to
whom one could speak in prayer', since, although there was
nobody actually 'on the other end of the line', the messages which
Jesus believed came down it were (van Buren surprisingly
asserts) concerned only with 'opportunities to serve, love, visit,
and clothe our neighbour'.[36] Dr. John Knox, in a remarkable re-
definition, is prepared to assert that Jesus is divine, provided that
divinity is taken as meaning 'a transformed, a redeemed and
redemptive *humanity*'; pre-existence of the person of Jesus is
explicitly excluded.[37] Dr. J. A. T. Robinson, while rejecting what
he calls 'the whole supranaturalistic scheme', writes that 'we
shall be grievously impoverished if our ears cannot tune to the
angels' song or our eyes are blind to the wise men's star. But we
must be able to read the nativity story without assuming that its

[36] *Theological Explorations* (New York: Macmillan, and London:
S.P.C.K., 1968), p. 179.

[37] *Humanity and Divinity of Christ* (Cambridge: University Press, 1967),
p. 113.

truth depends on their being a literal interruption of the natural by the supernatural.'[38] But the high tide of anti-supernaturalist reductionism is, I think, reached by Dr. Thomas Boslooper, who, having insisted that 'the virgin birth of Jesus ought to be maintained and believed in the twentieth century as it was in the first and second' and that 'the absence of the virgin birth in the contemporary Christian World Mission is unthinkable', reinterprets it as meaning 'that God acted in history and that monogamous marriage is civilization's most important social institution'.[39]

To play fast and loose with the accepted meanings of words in this way seems to me to be quite outrageous. It is a poisoning of the wells of language and makes intelligible communication between intelligent human beings virtually impossible. When employed in courts of law, this practice has frequently resulted in criminal proceedings. But its prevalence in modern theological writing testifies to two things: that without the use of the traditional supernaturalistic language it is extremely difficult to make Christian belief appear different from atheistic secularism, and that traditional Christian belief has a nostalgic character even for those who no longer hold it. The theological secularisers seem in fact to hover between two opposed ambitions: that of finding a way of expressing traditional Christian belief in entirely secularist language and concepts, and that of clothing atheistic secularism in the language of traditional Christianity. Dr. Robinson and Dr. Knox, I think, incline on the whole to the former; Dr. van Buren is clearly committed to the latter. But the thought of this school is so generally vague and its statements are so frequently

---

[38] *Honest to God* (London: S.C.M. Press, and Philadelphia: Westminster Press, 1963), p. 68.

[39] *The Virgin Birth* (London: S.C.M. Press, and Philadelphia: Westminster Press, 1962), pp. 232, 234.

ambiguous that it is not easy to gather with confidence what the precise position of any one of them is. What seems common to all of them is the uncriticized assumption that there is a radical antagonism between the very notions of the natural and the supernatural and that this is to be resolved only by abolishing or at any rate minimizing the supernatural. This is especially obvious in the realm of Christology; writers such as John Knox, J. A. T. Robinson, W. Norman Pittenger, and Piet Schoonenberg[40] all assume that to take the personal deity of Jesus literally is inevitably to devaluate his humanity; they therefore insist upon the reality and completeness of his humanity, and in this they are perfectly correct, but they mistakenly conclude that this is incompatible with the deity of his person. Thus we have Dr. Knox's notorious statement: 'We can have the humanity without the pre-existence and we can have the pre-existence without the humanity. There is absolutely no way of having both.'[41] Thus the humanity is emphasized and the deity is left to look after itself. And most of the old christological heresies appear in modern dress: adoptionism, Nestorianism, dynamic monarchianism, and the rest, and often with a very naturalistic or metaphorical interpretation of God himself. The same tendency is manifested in other topics wherein the divine and the human come into relation, that is, in almost the whole of Christian theology: salvation, grace, the beatific vision, all are denied or eviscerated, and the most that we are left with is some purely natural substitute bearing a usurped title. It is my chief purpose in these lectures to argue that this assumed antagonism between the

[40] John Knox, *Humanity and Divinity of Christ*; J. A. T. Robinson, *The Human Face of God*; W. N. Pittenger, *The Word Incarnate* and *Christology Reconsidered*; P. Schoonenberg, *The Christ*.

[41] *Humanity and Divinity of Christ*, p. 106.

natural and the supernatural is fallacious, and that the more God and the supernatural are emphasized the more clearly there appears the significance and dignity of the natural end of man. But to make this point we must discuss in detail the precise character of the relation between the orders of nature and supernature, and this involves discussing in detail the still profounder relation between the Creator and his creature, between God and man. This will be the subject of my third lecture. And there is another matter to which we must attend first.

The writers whom I have just mentioned reject the distinction between the natural and the supernatural because their outlook is entirely naturalistic and they wish therefore to abolish or at any rate to minimize the supernatural. There is, however, another school of thought which is highly suspicious of the distinction because they hold that the whole of man's being is infused and permeated with the supernatural and that the distinction suggests that there is an element of man—the natural—which is isolated from it. Thus, in spite of the fact that phrases such as *hyperousios* are common in the Greek fathers, one of the most original and stimulating of modern Russian theologians, Fr. Paul Evdokimov, has written as follows:

For Orthodox theology it is at its source that created nature sees grace as involved in the creative act itself. The absence of grace is not even thinkable, it would be a perversion that annihilated nature, equivalent to the second death in the Apocalypse. The truth of nature is to be supernature, where 'super' means deiform and theophoric in its very origins. It is in his essence that man is struck in the image of God, and it is this ontological deiformity that explains that grace is 'connatural' to nature, in the same way that nature is conformed to grace. They are complementary and compenetrate each other mutually: in participation, each exists in the other. . . . Man is created sharing in the nature of God (the *spiraculum vitae*), and God, in the incarnation, shares in human nature. To the deiformity of man there corresponds the humanity of God.[42]

It is therefore not surprising that Orthodox theologians make frequent use of the term *theandrism* or 'Godmanhood' to describe this mutual relationship of God and man, though most of them would not accept the view of it expounded in the last century by Vladimir Soloviev, in whose work, to quote another Russian Orthodox lay theologian, Vladimir Lossky, 'the mystical cosmology of Jacob Boehme, of Paracelsus and of the Kabbala are mixed up with the sociological ideas of Fourier and of Auguste Comte'.[43] Nor, I think, would most of them be at ease with the 'eternal Godmanhood' of Paul Tillich,[44] which has been searchingly criticized by Fr. George H. Tavard.[45]

Evdokimov locates his theme in the wider theological context in the following passage:

For Westerns, human nature comprises intellectual and animal life, and spiritual life (the supernatural) is superadded and in a certain measure superposed on a purely human economy. It is especially in reaction against Baianism (grace as an integral part of nature) and in Tridentine theology that the West conceives grace as extrinsic to the

[42] *L'Orthodoxie* (Neuchâtel: Delachaux et Niestlé, 1959), p. 88 (my translation).

[43] *The Mystical Theology of the Eastern Church* (Cambridge: James Clarke, 1957), p. 112. Soloviev's *Lectures on Godmanhood*, delivered during 1877–84, appeared in an English translation in London in 1948 (Dennis Dobson: London).

[44] *Systematic Theology*, II (Welwyn: Nisbet, 1968, and Chicago: University of Chicago Press, 1967), passim.

[45] *Paul Tillich and the Christian Message* (London: Burns & Oates, and New York: Scribner, 1962), pp. 169 ff. *et al.*

creature; the superposed supernatural shows nature in its very principle as strange to it. The Reformation takes up this outlook and out of
the supernatural grace of the scholastic makes an antinatural principle.
For Western asceticism, to follow nature is always to run counter to
grace. For the East, 'man in the image of God' defines exactly what man
is by nature. To be created in the image of God carries with it the grace
of this image, and this is why, for Eastern asceticism, to follow one's
true nature is to work in the direction of grace. Grace is connatural,
supernaturally natural to nature. Nature bears an innate exigency for
grace and this gift makes it charismatic from the start. The term 'supernatural' in Eastern mysticism is reserved for the supreme degree of
deification. The natural order is thus conformed to the order of grace,
is perfected in it and culminates in deifying grace.[46]

We shall have to see later on whether this account is entirely
fair to the Western tradition, especially in its description of the
Western Catholic position as extrinsecist; the report[47] of the
important conference on the theology of grace, held at Chevetogne in 1953 between Roman Catholics, Eastern Orthodox, and
Calvinists, used the term 'extrinsic' of the Protestant view, applying the terms 'created grace' and 'deification' to the Roman
Catholic and Orthodox views respectively. It is well, however, to
remember that the ascetic theology of East and West, like the
dogmatic theology, has been conducted in two very different
philosophical climates. If the Eastern emphasis upon deification
seems, not only to Protestants but also to some Western Catholics,
to verge upon pantheism, one must remember that the Eastern
statements have as their basis the Palamite doctrine that, while

[46] *L'Orthodoxie*, p. 90.
[47] C. Moeller and G. Philips, ed., *The Theology of Grace and the Oecumenical Movement* (London: Mowbrays, 1961), pp. 2 ff. *et al.* See also the
discussion in my *The Openness of Being*, Appendix III.

God is really communicated in his energies, his essence is altogether incommunicable; thus Vladimir Lossky writes:

> Western theology which, even in the doctrine of the Trinity, puts the emphasis upon the one essence, is even less prepared to admit any distinction between the essence and the energies. On the other hand, it establishes other distinctions foreign to Eastern theology: such as that between the light of glory and the light of grace—both created; and between other elements of the 'supernatural order' such as the gifts of the Holy Spirit, the infused virtues, and habitual and actual grace. Eastern tradition knows no such supernatural order between God and the created world, adding, as it were, to the latter a new creation. It recognizes no distinction, or rather division, save that between the created and the uncreated. For Eastern tradition the created supernatural has no existence. That which Western theology calls by the name of the *supernatural* signifies for the East the *uncreated*—the divine energies ineffably distinct from the essence of God.[48]

I have suggested elsewhere that when one gets behind words to their meanings there may be no fundamental, or at any rate no basic dogmatic, contradiction between the views of St. Gregory Palamas and St. Thomas Aquinas on this question,[49] but I cannot say more about it here; we may, however, notice that 'deification' and similar terms are by no means absent from the Western Catholic writers and indeed they have sometimes led Protestants to accuse Catholicism of being pantheistic! On the other hand, when the Orthodox are scandalized by the Western notion of 'created grace'—and this sometimes seems to be an even greater stumbling-block than the *Filioque*—it is pertinent to remark that since grace relates the Creator and the creature it must

[48] *The Mystical Theology of the Eastern Church*, p. 88.
[49] *Via Media* (London: Longmans Green, 1956, and Greenwich [Conn.]: The Seabury Press, 1957), Chap. iv. Cf. *The Openness of Being*, pp. 224 ff.

presumably have both an uncreated and a created aspect. It was remarked at Chevetogne that the notion of created grace, which in any case appears only towards the end of the twelfth century (the actual term 'created grace' seems first to occur in Alexander of Hales about 1245), was developed by such great scholastics as St. Bonaventura and St. Thomas Aquinas in order to exclude any Pelagian doctrine of human righteousness and to stress that grace produces a real change in man.[50] Recent Catholic theologians, such as Karl Rahner,[51] Piet Fransen,[52] and Robert W. Gleason[53]—all, as it happens, Jesuits—have thought along these lines, and Gleason categorically remarks that the difference between East and West 'is a distinction not of opposition but of emphasis only, based on a different philosophical orientation'.[54] But now we must look at the outstanding contribution made to this whole question by the learned and brilliant French Jesuit Fr. Henri de Lubac.

Fr. de Lubac's relevant writings are to be found in the three volumes *Surnaturel*, published in 1946, *Augustinisme et théologie moderne* and *Le Mystère du surnaturel*, the last two published in

[50] *The Theology of Grace and the Oecumenical Movement*, pp. 16 ff.; *The Openness of Being*, pp. 224 ff.

[51] *Theological Investigations*, Vol. I, C. Ernst, trans. (London: Darton, Longman & Todd, 1966, and Baltimore: Hellicon, 1961), Chs. ix and x; Vol. IV, K. Smyth, trans. (London: Darton, Longman & Todd, 1967, and Baltimore: Helicon, 1967), Ch. vii; *Nature and Grace*, D. Wharton, trans. (London: Sheed & Ward, 1963, and New York: Sheed & Ward, 1964), pp. 3 ff.

[52] *The New Life of Grace*, G. Dupont, trans. (London: G. Chapman, 1969, and Greenwich Conn.: The Seabury Press, 1972), pp. 87 ff. *et al.*

[53] *Grace* (London: Sheed & Ward, 1962, and New York: Sheed & Ward, 1959), App. III *et al.*

[54] *Ibid.*, p. 223.

1965, and in English translations under the titles *Augustinianism and Modern Theology* and *The Mystery of the Supernatural*, in 1969 and 1967 respectively. The ultimate problem with which he was concerned goes right back to the Middle Ages; it is that of reconciling the natural ordination of man to the vision of God with the sheer gratuitousness of the grace by which alone he can achieve it. Man has a natural desire for a supernatural end, an end which can be achieved only by supernatural means. It is, however, impossible that God would leave a natural desire unfulfilled, therefore he would seem at least morally bound to grant the grace to achieve it. Therefore this grace would seem to be something other than a sheer, unconstrained gift from God, something which man could at the very least expect to receive, and indeed have in principle a right to claim.

It may be doubted whether St. Thomas saw this as a serious problem; this may be why scholars have found it so difficult to decide precisely what his solution to it was. Dr. Patrick K. Bastable's book *Desire for God* was published in 1947, but without reference to de Lubac; Fr. James E. O'Mahoney's book *The Desire for God in the Philosophy of St. Thomas Aquinas* had already appeared in 1929. De Lubac's immediate target was the doctrine of 'pure nature' which was elaborated by Roman Catholic theologians in reply to the errors of Baius and Jansen, who were believed to hold that in man's primitive state innocence and the clear vision of God were not a supernatural gift but a necessary complement of human nature itself. Thus the doctrine was formulated that man, by his nature, is a finite being who could be satisfied with a finite end, a purely natural beatitude; it is traced back to Cajetan, who, in this as in other matters today, appears not so much as the Prince of Commentators as the Angelic Doctor's first great perverter. As an appendix to his historical account of the question, Fr. de Lubac gives a very full exposition of the pre-history and history of the word 'supernatural' itself.[55] He traces the expressions *hyper physin* and *supra naturam* right back into patristic times, and the word *supernaturalis* to Isidore of Pelusium, who died *c.* 450. In the thirteenth century he says it became current, and he instances St. Albert and St. Thomas, but Dr. M. E. Dahl seems to be going too far when he says 'the very word is practically a coinage of St. Thomas Aquinas'.[56]

Dom Illtyd Trethowan has stated the matter very clearly in a review of the last two mentioned books of Fr. de Lubac:

> The theologian who adopts the new system, while admitting that a state of pure nature has never existed historically, nevertheless thinks of man as built up in two parts: a 'nature' to which a natural end corresponds and a 'supernature' to which a supernatural end corresponds. The two parts were no doubt created contemporaneously, but they are in themselves distinct from one another. God might have finished man off on the natural level instead of ordering him to a further end—and he would still be man. His natural desire, then, can only be for a natural happiness, whatever that can prove to mean (it proves to mean a large number of very different and very curious things). A desire for the supernatural can arise only if a further end is super-added. Man, in fact, could get along perfectly well in his own way if God had left him to it. And God begins to look like a tiresome intruder upon man's peace of mind. It should not be necessary to point out the implications of this point of view. But it may still need to be emphasized that when there is talk of a 'supernatural order' as though it were an 'extra', something laid on top of a 'natural order', there must inevitably be competition and collision between the two. Unless nature is conceived of not merely statically but also dynamically, as *ordered to* the supernatural, there can be no true Christian

[55] *Surnaturel* (Paris: Aubier, 1946), pp. 325 ff.
[56] *The Resurrection of the Body* (London: Allenson & Co., 1962), p. 48.

anthropology. And so it is fitting that the famous last chapter of *Surnaturel* should contain in its first paragraph a quotation from Blondel's *L'Action*.[57]

It is, I think, clear that the 'Western' doctrine which the Eastern Orthodox theologians have found so abhorrent is in fact the 'new system' of pure nature to which de Lubac is equally opposed. Evdokimov was right in seeing it as a reaction against Baianism, though he seemed to think that it was more deeply rooted in Roman Catholicism than later developments have shown it to be. De Lubac himself sees his attitude as a movement back to Augustine and Aquinas, but also as coherent with the tradition of Greek Christianity.

> The essence of this 'Augustinianism' applies as much to the great scholastics of the thirteenth century as to Augustine himself, and one would not wish to lose the advantage of any of their clarifications. It applies also, as I have said, to the Greek tradition; it is not linked exclusively with the thought of Augustine, and the greater example of Thomas Aquinas shows that it can be well integrated with an Aristotelianism transformed by the principles that underlie all Christian philosophy

But, he adds—and this is of first importance,

> St. Augustine and many of his disciples generally lumped together two problems which we have long since learned to separate—and which in fact the Greek doctors who came after Irenaeus separated—the problem of the final end, and that of man's initial equipment for the journey to salvation.[58]

And it is interesting that de Lubac, towards the end of his work, makes an approving, though passing, reference to Palamas, which

[57] *Downside Review*, 85 (1966), 399 f.

[58] *The Mystery of the Supernatural*, Rosemary Sheed, trans. (London: Geoffrey Chapman, and New York: Herder & Herder, 1967), pp. 21 f.

leaves one wishing that he had followed it up in detail. But he makes also a protest against mere archaism, which one would wish to recommend to the Orthodox, with their tremendous respect for tradition and the Fathers:

> Archaism . . . is as illusory, in the reverse sense, as the idea of inevitable progress. . . . To refer to the ancients, said Cassiodorus, enables us to escape from all kinds of objections and difficulties. And there are some 'difficulties' that face us from which we ought not and cannot escape. The passing of time has brought to light deviations and errors, sometimes of the greatest subtlety, which we must meet with an equal subtlety and exactness. . . . In this sense it is true to say that we never retrace our steps. We never return to the past. Our faith is not old, is not something of the past: it is eternal, and always new.[59]

Time is insufficient for me to give an adequate discussion or even a full exposition of Fr. de Lubac's position; I can only indicate what seem to me to be its most significant features. First of all, he is explicit that he is dealing with a mystery, in the strict theological sense of that word; the title of his work, *The Mystery of the Supernatural*, indicates this. He is not professing to give neat answers to all conceivable questions, but to help us to penetrate a little further into the fathomless depths of God who is love. Secondly, while repudiating the doctrine of the two ends of man as it was held by the pure-nature school, he is uncompromising on the sheer gratuitousness of man's supernatural end and of the grace by which he can achieve it. And he is able to do this because his view of man is thoroughly dynamic.

> The 'close accord' and the kind of 'continuity' summed up in the axiom (stated of old by William of Auxerre and William of Auvergne) *gratia perficit naturam* or *gratia proportionatur naturae ut perfectio perfec-*

[59] *Ibid.*, p. 23.

tibili, or again *natura praeambula est ad gratiam* by no means preclude, from another aspect, the total transcendence of the supernatural gift, its perfect spontaneity, and its difference in kind from 'nature'.[60]

Again, while admitting that there are certain general principles, such as those just quoted, relating grace to nature as such, de Lubac is emphatic that, because men and angels are a very special kind of creature and because man is made in the image of God, grace will have certain relations to them that it does not have to creatures in general. He writes:

If, then there is a human nature and an angelic nature, we cannot use the terms *wholly* in the sense in which we speak of animal nature, for instance, or cosmic nature. If every created spirit, before being a thinking spirit, is itself 'nature', if, before even being thinking, 'it is spiritual nature', then it must also be recognized that, in another sense, spirit is in contrast with 'nature'.[61]

St. Augustine is quoted as saying that 'man alone, of all the beings in the world, is capable of beatitude',[62] and Duns Scotus as saying that 'man's end is natural to him if considered in terms of his desire, but supernatural in terms of how it is attained, or by whom it is brought about'.[63] There is also an extremely illuminating remark, which may help to dispose of the objection that, although theologians say that all men have by nature a desire for the vision of God, there does not seem to be a great deal of empirical evidence for this. Fr. de Lubac says:

I do not say that the knowledge gained by reason of a natural desire, outside any context of faith, 'proves strictly that we are called to the

[60] *Ibid.*, pp. 30f.
[61] *Ibid.*, p. 133.
[62] *Ibid.*, p. 137.
[63] *Ibid.*, pp. 150f.

beatific vision', and that therefore we can naturally attain 'the certainty that we have been created for that end'; on the contrary, I say that the knowledge that is revealed to us of that calling, which makes us certain of that end leads us to recognize within ourselves the existence and nature of that desire.[64]

And he stresses the radical difference between the ancient Greek and the Christian view of human beatitude.

Aristotle's thought marked an advance on that of his master. For him the supreme principle is no longer the objectified idea, but a living mind, the supreme intelligence, and also the supreme intelligible, 'thought of thought' . . .; but that eternal and perfect living being is eternally unaware of us imperfect beings. . . . But since the time of Plato and Aristotle, a 'light has shone in our sky', and all is new. . . . The 'beatific vision' is no longer the contemplation of a spectacle, but an intimate participation in the vision the Son has of the Father in the bosom of the Trinity. Revelation, by making us know in his Son the God of Love, the personal and trinitarian God, the creating and saving God, the God 'who was made man to make us God', has changed everything.[65]

Fr. de Lubac does not profess to solve all the problems, but I think we may justly say that most of them fall into the background or are radically transformed in the light of his stress upon the essentially dynamic character of God's grace and upon the fact that God is trinitarian Love, who has made us and preserves us in his image and calls us to enjoy his own trinitarian life. It is because of this that he can at the end of his argument so uncompromisingly and repeatedly declare the absolute and unqualified gratuitousness of grace and the supernatural order,

[64] *Ibid.*, p. 274.
[65] *Ibid.*, pp. 298 f.

without having to postulate for man a natural as well as a super-natural end.[66] An Eastern Orthodox who had followed him to this point might perhaps say that de Lubac had really shown that the distinction between the natural and the supernatural was cumbersome and otiose, but I do not think he would be right in so saying. For, however much we stress the singleness of the end to which God has called man, there is surely a distinction between God's calling man into being as an inhabitant of 'this world', equipped with the necessities for living 'this life', and God's calling him to enjoy eternal life in the blessed Trinity, endowed with the graces for attaining this end. I see no reason why the differences between East and West on this question of grace should not yield to serious and constructive dialogue, now that Fr. de Lubac's demolition of the 'pure nature' theory has become generally accepted.

[66] *Ibid.*, pp. 309 f.

LECTURE TWO: DISCUSSION

Question 1:

Could you perhaps briefly explain what you consider to be the basic relevance of the nature-grace problematic in contemporary theology?

Mascall:

I think that it is only through Christ that men are saved. On the other hand, I think that it is equally possible for those who have not heard of Christ to be saved. This does mean that the grace of Christ can probably be found even where it is in fact not recognized. In trying to deal with that fact one is dealing with the relation between grace and nature.

I think another point in which this comes in is in the fact that we must, if we are honest, affirm the goodness of man's natural activities. They can, of course, be perverted. I think we must assert that the things which man does in this world, in this life, making use of the various means with which God has equipped him and of the discoveries and the inventiveness of scientists and technologists, man's concern with himself in this life and this world—these are a good thing. At the same time we are bound to say that God intends us not simply to be happy with things in this world and this life but to achieve life with him in the beatific vision. Therefore, it seems to me again a question of nature and grace, or nature and supernature.

Many of you know of Karl Barth with his extremely laudable emphasis upon the fact that it is only through Christ that we can be saved. He proposed a theology of grace which does not have any kind of organic relationship between grace and nature, and looks upon everything man does apart from his response in faith to God as being perverted. So it does seem to me that this question is one of considerable importance for the Church in the present day, and it comes in when questions about the salvation of non-believers and the Church's position in the age of scientific discovery are raised.

Question 2:

You define 'nature' and 'supernature' in your second lecture as: 'If, then, there are any aspects of man and his activity which are not concerned simply with "this life", or which, even during "this life", are not concerned simply with "this world", they may legitimately be termed "supernatural"'. I wonder if it is a good and fruitful idea to try to get a definition that both secularists and Christians agree upon as some sort of lowest common denominator that both of them would accept. Is it not rather up to the Christian Church with its theologians to define what nature and supernature are, both in a descriptive manner and in an explanatory manner?

Mascall:

I would like to clarify what I said. I didn't mean to suggest that
the way to get a satisfactory definition of nature and supernature
was for Christians and secularists to meet together and try to
hammer out a definition. I think the definition of nature and
supernature is one which the Church has to give from its own
knowledge of God's dealings with man. But I think that when
that has been done, Christians can in fact make use of these
definitions in talking with secularists. I do not think that it is
from the dialogue with the secularists that the Christian derives
an understanding of grace and nature, but I think that from his
own understanding of his faith and the resulting definitions that
he does in fact have a point from which he can start. I don't
think you have this point of departure if you start off with, say,
Karl Barth's definition or understanding of what grace and nature
are.

Question 3:

There is great stress today in such theologians as Karl Rahner and
Bernard Lonergan on the experience of grace. Lonergan, for
example, speaks of the experience of being in love in an unrestricted fashion as an experience of grace in the psychological
order. What is your position on the question of the experience of
grace?

Mascall:

That's a difficult question and I am not confident I have the
answer. I am perhaps a little bit surprised to find theologians

such as Karl Rahner appearing to treat grace as though it were something on the purely psychological level. I don't think they mean that, but they do, I think, assert that if grace is not something simply on the psychological level, it ought nevertheless to be discerned there rather more than in the manner traditional Christian theology, especially Catholic theology, has usually supposed it to be. I don't think that there is a fundamental difference between their position and mine. I certainly do not want to say that grace is so much limited to the ontological level that it doesn't produce any effects on the psychological level at all. I am not going to that. I shall point out in my third lecture, that when St. Thomas says that grace is not something in the virtues but something in the essence of the soul, it is not suggested that grace is not manifested through the virtues, but that grace is something which operates, so to speak, in the very deepest level of man, at the point where he is given his existence by God and not at the level of feelings or impulses, even of volitions. And so I would say that grace is something on the ontological level, something where God touches man's very existence, but that it does produce its effects on the level of feelings and of behaviour. On the basic point I don't think I differ much from Rahner and Lonergan.

Question 4:

Do you think that the best way to approach the grace problematic is from a definition in a synthetic fashion? What would you say of Lonergan's approach in *Insight* where he exposes the problem of evil and the possible solution of grace?

Mascall:

I think I would probably answer to that by recalling the monk who spread out his cowl on the floor and crawled into it: that's one way of doing it. And Lonergan's way of approaching this matter is one which he works out with tremendous skill and in tremendous detail. The main reason, I think, why I gave the kind of definition I did of nature and, consequently, of super-nature and grace is because purely on the empirical level, man is a member of this world, living this life, and it is possible for him to organize his behaviour as if this life and this world were all that there are. I know, of course, as a Christian that this world and this life are not the sum of reality. But it seems to me that one must have a definition of nature and grace which enables one to recognize that a person who is living this life in this world is in fact doing something it is possible for human beings to do; and in fact, even if he responds supernaturally, he still has to live this life in this world. The kind of definition I give of nature is an empirical one, a working one, and I think that if one doesn't clarify one's basic meaning of nature and supernature, one will either be left with a term 'nature' which does not have any or-ganic connection with grace or else one will simply confuse the two.

Question 5:

Do you think it is possible to differentiate within one's conscious psychological experience between elements of nature and ele-ments of grace, or are the two so intimately conjoined that no differentiation is possible?

Mascall:

I think it is possible to a limited extent. The first question, of course, is whether this attempt to differentiate in someone's conscious experience between the elements of nature and grace is being done by the person himself or by somebody else. In neither case can you lay down an absolute hard and fast rule. If we try to examine our own psychological condition, it is doubtful whether we are sufficiently detached from ourselves, but if somebody else is doing it, then he has only an external point of view. But having said that, I would have thought that it is possible, making all the allowances for the limitations of human fallibility, that one can sometimes see in some particular thing one did, some act one performed, that one's own powers were assisted by grace. And I think it is possible with the same limitations to see in somebody else's behaviour evidence which seems to correspond to the same situation.

But this is all extremely tentative, because one of the ways in which God does in fact act upon us is not by suppressing our natural powers, but by releasing them. And so one does sometimes discern grace in somebody else simply by noting the extent to which are manifested certain active conditions to a greater extent than is normal. By and large, one is able to say sometimes that God's grace was in fact operative, but always with this limitation of the fallibility of our judgment upon it.

Question 6:

I would preface a single question with perhaps a questionable suggestion on the term 'supernature'. It seems to me that the ambiguity may be greater than if one used the term 'transnature'. Are you rejecting any generic or functional relationship, yet apparently permitting a causal relationship between the two, if not generally, at least at times? I was wondering if you are not accepting some sort of general relationship. My question is, in the light of this acceptance of nature, in whatever occurs, to what extent do the Baconian and Darwinian revolution and the scientific aspects of modern technology and psychological behaviour today, existentialism and the theology of the death of God, influence our notion of grace and nature?

Mascall:

'Supernature' is the term I use, but I think that 'transnature' could be used. I do think that it is extremely important for us to take into account modern science, evolution, politics, biology, psychology, sociology, and most other things. The basic question seems to me that what in fact science has shown to us is simply what nature is, what human nature is. I don't think it throws any particular light on the question of the relation between nature and grace. There is obviously a problem how natural forces, whether they are manifested in inanimate objects or in animals or in man, are related to God. St. Thomas says God moves all creatures according to what they are; he moves natural causes according to the nature of natural causes and voluntary ones according to the nature of voluntary causes. This is what the situation is. But how one explains this depends upon what one thinks explanation is.

I think a tremendous amount of confusion is caused by assuming that if a man is to be free in some area then somehow God must withdraw himself from that particular area in order for a man to be free. I think the exact opposite is the case. It is in giving him freedom that God enters into the situation and by his activity that he makes man free. This is paradoxical; but I think this is the way persons act upon persons. Take the idealized situation of the perfect tutor and the perfect pupil. If the tutor is really performing his task, then the relationship is not that the tutor does all the work and the pupil does none. It is in fact the influence of the tutor on the pupil that helps the pupil to be what he is. It is neither that the tutor overrides the pupil's freedom, nor that he just sits back and waits. This is also true between God and human beings. And along that line I cannot see that the 'death of God' conclusion really follows at all. God has made beings which have real powers and energies, and at the same time God is perpetually preserving them with those powers and energies. I think that is my general answer.

Question 7:

To what extent do you place importance on the sacramental rite of baptism as a cause of the actualization of supernatural life in man?

Mascall:

I think, of course, that baptism like the other sacraments is of the supernatural order. They are concerned with man's life in God and not simply with prosperity, comfort, and so on, in this life in this world. So it seems to me that the whole supernatural structure of the Christian religion is a powerful sign of the grace-giving activity of God. The sacramental economy is something which depends on how God has arranged it. God has arranged things in a way which corresponds to our needs, our capacities, and so on. I do not think that what I am suggesting in any way conflicts with the traditional views about the sacraments. There are persons with other views, and they have sometimes thought of the sacraments in isolation from one another and in isolation from the Church as the body of Christ and the whole redemptive act of God in Christ. What I would say about sacramental theology reinforces the traditional notion.

I'll sum it up in this way: if the sacraments are a means of grace, then how will that grace also come to people outside the sacraments? To ask this will illuminate our understanding both of grace and of the sacraments God has given us.

3

NATURE AND GRACE

It can hardly have escaped the attention of my hearers that, while I have given a fairly precise definition of the nouns 'nature' and 'supernature' and of the corresponding adjectives 'natural' and 'supernatural', I have allowed the meaning of the word 'grace' to appear only by implication. It is not, in fact, my intention to discuss systematically the various nuances which the notion of grace has acquired in the course of Christian history: healing grace and elevating grace, justifying grace and sanctifying grace, operative grace and co-operative grace, sufficient grace and efficacious grace, habitual grace and actual grace, uncreated grace and created grace; all these dualities and contrasts arise from the mysterious truth that grace relates personal God and personal man. In the sense with which I am concerned it will perhaps be sufficient to define grace as that relation of God towards man which is involved in man's supernatural, as distinct from his natural, life. This does not imply that grace is not involved in man's redemption and restoration from his fallen condition, but it does mean that, in redeeming and restoring man, God has in view not merely the replacement of man in a purely natural state but the relocating of him on the way that leads to

the beatific vision. This will become more understandable if we
recognize that man's natural orientation to a supernatural end
does not conflict with the sheer gratuitousness of the grace which
God gives for its attainment. Nor does it prejudge the question
whether, in restoring man, God gives him an even more exalted
status than he could have achieved if he had never fallen. In the
words of Faber's famous hymn:

> 'Tis not all we owe to Jesus,
>   It is something more than all,
> Greater good because of evil,
>   Larger mercy through the fall.

Nor, I think, need we be worried at this time of day by the
question which so obsessed the men of the sixteenth and seven-
teenth centuries, whether grace, *charis*, *gratia*, implies a simple
change in God's attitude towards man, in virtue of which God
treats him as innocent while leaving him corrupt, or whether it
produces a real change in its recipient. Because God's word is
creative, what God says goes; it produces effects and does not
merely register attitudes. We have, I hope got far enough away
from late medieval nominalism to conceive of a real change in
man which is not simply reducible to an instantaneous change in
his perceptible behaviour. Again, I do not think we should take
too seriously the common accusation that the traditional ways of
talking about grace treat it as analogous to a medicine or some
other material substance that can be poured out of a bottle or
injected into the veins; this seems to me to rest upon a simple
fallacy about the function of abstract nouns in speech and of abstract concepts in thought. When a man is said to have fallen in
love, nobody supposes that falling in love is like falling into the
Potomac or the Ganges; if he is said to have flown into a rage,

nobody supposes that he had first to find a rage and then fly into it. So, when we use such phrases as 'finding grace', 'falling from grace', 'being in a state of grace', no materialistic or quasi-materialistic implications should be suspected unless we have totally lost consciousness of the fact that we are persons living in personal relationship with a personal—or, more exactly, a tri-personal—God.

When, for example, St. Thomas tells us that grace puts something in the soul (*ponit aliquid in anima*), that it is not a virtue, and that its subject is not one of the powers of the soul but the soul's essence,[67] what he is anxious to make clear is that grace is not a mere influence operating on a comparatively superficial level but is concerned with the deepest reality of man at the point where the Creator gives him his very being and conserves him in existence. And even when the limitations of his Aristotelian psychology lead the Angelic Doctor to describe grace as a quality,[68] he knows that it is a quality of a very special kind, by which the rational creature is raised above its natural condition to participate in the divine goodness.[69] Most of the time, it is true, he is speaking of that created grace which scandalizes the Orthodox; nevertheless he is not oblivious of its divine aspect. 'When a man is said to have God's grace,' he writes, 'something supernatural is referred to, issuing in man from God. Sometimes, however, by the grace of God is meant God's own eternal love (*ipsa aeterna Dei dilectio*).'[70] As I have previously said, grace, simply because it relates the Creator and the creature, must have both an uncreated and a created aspect; and, although the medie-

[67] *S. Theol.* I–II, cx, 1, 3, 4.
[68] *Ibid.*, 2.
[69] *Ibid.*
[70] *Ibid.*, 1c.

vals describe grace as a possession, a *habitus*, we must not forget
St. Bonaventure's assertion, *Habere est haberi*, which we might
paraphrase as 'To possess grace is to be possessed by God.'[71]

It is, I think, unfortunate that the Latin manuals have treated
actual grace before habitual or sanctifying grace; their excuse no
doubt lies in their concern to exclude Pelagianism. It is interesting
to see that Fr. Gleason, in company with other modern writers,
reverses this order, emphasizing that by grace 'man is made a
sharer in the divine nature and an adopted son of God' and that
this means 'that man has some kind of real participation in the
nature of God'.[72] (N.B. What is nature for God is supernature for
man.)

At the end of the last lecture I drew the distinction, which I
alleged to be significant, between God's calling man into being
as an inhabitant of 'this world', equipped with the necessities for
living 'this life', and God's calling him to eternal life in the
Blessed Trinity, endowed with the grace for attaining this latter
state. In the words of Emile Mersch:

> The infinite Being has two ways of giving himself to finite beings;
> by the former, he gives himself to them in *their* way, which makes
> them themselves; by the latter he gives himself to them in *his* way,
> which makes them one with him.[73]

To say this is not to deny that, even as an inhabitant of 'this
world', man is in intimate relation with God, that, as the pro-
logue to St. John's Gospel says, 'what was made was life in him'.[74]

---

[71] *Breviloquium*, 5, 1 quoted in *The Theology of Grace and the Oecumenical Movement*, p. 18.

[72] *Grace* (New York: Sheed & Ward, 1962), p. 72.

[73] 'Filii in Filio', *Nouvelle Revue Théologique*, 65 (1938), p. 825 (my translation).

[74] Jn 1 : 3–4 (the more probable rendering).

Mersch describes the 'first way' as *God giving himself*. Nor does it imply that, even in 'this world', man is limited to 'this life'. It does, however, mean that we must consider what is involved in man's existence as a member of the created world, before we go on to consider his elevation into the life of God by grace.

We must, in the first place, disown the type of emphasis upon God's transcendence which thinks of his creative act as launching into existence a world with which God has henceforth no genuine relationship; in whatever sense we are to accept St. Thomas's dictum that the relation between God and the world is real in the world but notional in God,[75] it cannot be that; and we must remember his complementary assertion that God is in all things by essence, power and presence.[76] It is, however, the view set forth in Dr. Harvey Cox's book *The Secular City*; for it, the de-divinization of the world which was the achievement of Judaeo-Christian religion means that not only is the world not God but that it has no real relation to him. Everything in the world happens as if there were no God and, although man has been set over it to dominate it and transform it, he is to dominate it and transform it as if God did not exist. In a very different context the same view turns up in the French writer Henry Duméry. For him, God, who resides in a realm of unknowability and inaccessibility like that of the One of Plotinus, has endowed man with such an absolute autonomy that he has to create his own values and live his own life as if there were no God at all. Like Sartre, Duméry believes in man's absolute self-creativity and autonomy, but whereas Sartre holds that this necessitates the non-existence of God, Duméry holds that it necessitates his existence. Philosophy cannot attain to God, but it can study religion as

[75] *S. Theol.* I, xlv, 3 ad I.
[76] *Ibid.*, viii, 3.

a phenomenon in human history. Thus, in Dr. Louis Dupré's words, 'Although there is no God of the philosophers, the God of religion is not inaccessible to philosophy.'[77]

Against all such deistic or quasi-deistic views, it must be asserted that the absolute distinction that there is between God and the world necessitates that the world is in the most intimate relation with him, a relation of complete dependence. As I expounded at length in my Gifford Lectures, *The Openness of Being*:

> . . . while exerting concrete existence and manifesting the special characteristics of the particular beings and kinds of being that each of them is, creatures are metaphysically incomplete and exist at all only because they are the objects of incessant creative activity on the part of God. They are centres of real existential energy, but this energy is finite and received; they have real determinate natures, but their natures are inherently limited and restricted in their sphere.

> [But] just because their being is both received and limited, it is inherently open to fresh influxes of creative activity from God. The view of the world that derives from these considerations is radically and uncompromisingly dynamic, and it stands in sharp contrast with the view that was typical of the ancient world. Greek philosophy, when it did not resolve the world into a featureless Heraclitean mush in which 'all things flow', thought of every being as a limited incapsulated entity, all of whose potentialities were included in it at the start, even if their development took time and was conditioned by their environment. . . . Over against this ultimately cramped and static view Christian philosophers developed the doctrine that finite beings are maintained and energized by the incessant creative activity of a personal God, who is himself infinite plenitude of activity . . . and who is continually pouring being into his creatures.[78]

[77] Introduction to Henry Duméry, *Faith and Reflection* (Evanston: Northwestern University, 1964), p. xix.

[78] Pp. 145 f.

Old habits die hard, and even Christian philosophers have not always resisted the temptation to fall back into the way of thinking of creatures as self-enclosed though limited entities, preserved and supported by God indeed, but capable of further concern on his part only in so far as they may be externally manipulated by him or used by him as a substratum on which he erects a supernatural superstructure of grace. Now it is my contention that even God himself could not create beings of this type, since self-sufficiency and self-inclusiveness are inconsistent with finitude and creaturehood. A creature, that is to say a being that is both real and contingent, can only exist in open orientation to him who is its creative source and who therefore can bestow upon it fresh and unanticipable modes of operation and can actualize hitherto undiscerned and unpredictable potentialities. Thus, we must understand the accepted maxim that nature has a pure *potentia oboedientialis* for grace in the most dynamic way; not admittedly, that nature can actualize its own potentialities, but that its own potentialities—its God-given potentialities—are what grace actualizes in it. Thus we can see how it is possible for man to have by nature an orientation to the beatific vision, although the satisfaction of that orientation can be achieved only by grace. But here there is a further clarification to be made.

I do not believe that it is only in relation to grace and the supernatural that the openness of nature to the creative activity of God appertains; it applies on the level of nature itself. That is to say, it is not involved only in man's elevation into the life of God and his attainment of eternal beatitude, but also to his living of 'this life' in 'this world' and to this world in which he lives it. It is a violation of the truth about both man and the world to assume that man has two unrelated and unconnected lives to live, a natural life which he can live simply by drawing on the ontological capital with which God initially endowed him, without further commerce with its donor, and a supernatural life which he can live only by the grace of God. Simply as a creature, man is open to, and in need of, fresh influxes of creative activity on the part of the creator. And, in various modes and degrees, this is true also of the world in which man lives and of which, in virtue of his bodily aspect, he is in fact a part. It is along this line that I suggest we should conceive of that activity of God in the whole evolutionary process on which many modern Christian writers have laid stress. I do not think that everything that they have written has been balanced and accurate, and I am far from wishing to hitch the wagon of the Christian faith to the supernovas of contemporary scientific theories, but I think we may say that the outlook of modern science, in contrast with that of the eighteenth and nineteenth centuries, has largely freed itself from its former bonds and no longer assumes that science is possible only in a setting of rigid determinism. However, I cannot enter here into a discussion of Einstein, Huxley, Freud and Monod. I would, nevertheless, suggest that some of the difficulties which responsible Christian thinkers have had in giving unqualified endorsement to the insights of Pierre Teilhard de Chardin might have been considerably diminished if the great Jesuit mystic had prefaced the development of his cosmological and biological insights with a thorough consideration of the character of the world's relation to its creator and of the mutual relation of the orders of nature and grace.

I must answer an objection which may well have been provoked by the assertions which I have just made. If the principle that created being is essentially open to unforeseeable and undemandable fresh influxes of divine creative action holds within the level of nature itself and not only in the elevation of nature to supernature, has not the distinction between the two orders been virtually abolished? Was it not the definition of the natural life that it could be lived without grace, and the definition of the supernatural life that it could not? My reply is that these were not in fact the definitions of the two orders, but that the orders are none the less distinct. I did not define the natural life of man as life that was isolated from fresh creative divine activity, but as life that was concerned simply with 'this world' and with the period between conception in the womb and bodily death. And I did not define the supernatural life as life that could only be lived by grace—though I hold that to be true—but as life which is lived in God and is orientated to the beatific vision. And, while these two orders are clearly distinct, they are intimately related, if only because it is the same human being who can live both. The famous Thomist texts make this clear. 'Grace does not take away nature but perfects it';[79] 'Grace presupposes nature';[80] 'Grace is proportioned to nature as the perfector to the perfectible';[81] and 'Nature is the preamble to grace.'[82] It is clear that in St. Thomas's mind not only does nature need grace if its possibilities are to be realized, but also grace needs nature as the material in which it is to work. Without nature, grace would be left in a vacuum and would be an unreal fiction, for the function of grace is to supernaturalize nature. Or, in less abstract language, grace elevates man into the life of God.

I have just said that nature needs grace if its possibilities are to be realized; I did not say *all* its possibilities. For if it is of the very

[79] *S. Theol.* I, i, 8 ad 2; cf. *De Ver.*, xxvi, 6 ad 1.
[80] *S. Theol.* I, ii, 2 ad 1.
[81] *De Ver.*, xxvii, 5, obj. 7.
[82] *In Boet.* de Trin., ii, 3.

essence of a creature to be open to God, there can be no ante-cedently specifiable limits to the graces God can give it; even when he has raised it to share in his own life, it is still finite, still a creature, and there is no upper limit to finitude. As the mathe-maticians tell us, there is no greatest finite quantity. No doubt, *quidquid recipitur recipitur ad modum recipientis*, and perhaps even in the beatific vision, when God is seen *totum sed non totaliter*, one star will differ from another in glory. And, as A. E. Taylor once suggested, even in heaven there may be progress in beatitude, though no longer progress towards it.[83] Be that as it may, while we are on our pilgrimage, *in via*, there are no theoretical limits to the graces that God *can* give, for whatever graces he has given he can always give more. Man's capacity to receive, his *potentia oboedientalis* for grace, is unlimited, except in so far as it is blocked by sin, and so is God's capacity to give. On the other hand, the graces that he has already given are more than we could either expect or demand. And what makes a man blessed is not that all his potentialities are actualized—that may in any case, be a logical or metaphysical impossibility—but that those are actualized which God, in his wisdom, sees fit to actualize. The Christian life has thus the extremely exhilarating character that in it unlimited gratitude is combined with unexpected surprises. For neither in the order of nature nor in the order of grace does God just act once and no more. 'Of his fullness we have all received,' writes St. John, 'and one grace after another,' *charin anti charitos*.[84]

I do not think that we can dispense with the distinction between nature and supernature, for, as Mersch maintained, God gives

[83] *The Faith of a Moralist*, The Gifford Lectures 1926–1928 (New York and London: Macmillan, 1930; one vol. edition 1937), I, ch. ix.

[84] Jn. 1:16.

himself to us in two ways, one that makes us ourselves to live in our way and one that makes us one with him to live in his. And, although a life lived deliberately simply on the level of nature is arid and cramped, shutting its eyes to the grace that God offers and ignoring the fact that it bears within itself a hunger that it cannot satisfy, nature has nevertheless its own natural desires, finalities, and operations, which must not be spurned at the behest of an allegedly more spiritual view of man. But in the last resort man's failure not just to solve, for that is not surprising in a fallen world, but even to understand the nature of his personal, social, economic, and political problems arises from his unreadiness to accept the fundamental truth that he has a natural desire that nature cannot satisfy.

The complaints that the Eastern Orthodox bring against the Western doctrine of nature and supernature are valid against the view of 'pure nature' which the West is in course of abandoning. But I do not think that their own formulations do justice to the complexities of man's being and of the human situation *in via*. In the political sphere, the inadequacies of the Western 'pure nature' view have led to an artificial separation of the realms of Church and State, so that when the two come into collision each tends simply to demand the functions of the other; either the Church demands recognition as a political entity or the State claims recognition as divine. On the other hand, the Eastern view has tended to fuse together Church and State so that the Church tends to lose any power of judgment and discrimination in the moral, and specially in the political, life of the community.

With the abandonment of the 'pure nature' view in the West the way should be open for constructive dialogue on the theological plane. Fr. de Lubac with immense courage made the

breakthrough, which later writers such as Karl Rahner have fruit-
fully exploited.[85] Thus Rahner has criticized the text-book view
on several grounds: first, that it assumes we know *precisely* what
human nature is like; secondly, that it makes man's supernatural
vocation and the gift of grace a kind of *disturbance* rather than a
fulfilment of his nature; thirdly that, if what man concretely *is*
depends utterly on God, we cannot admit that God's ordination of
him to a supernatural end is simply a juridical decree and does not
penetrate to man's ontological depths. Unfortunately, Rahner's
own discussion is extremely involved; I have tried to disentangle
it in an appendix to my book *The Openness of Being*. I am not
convinced that his introduction of the notion of a 'supernatural
existential' adds very much to the discussion, but his insistence
upon the fact that 'nature', as contrasted with the supernatural, is
a 'remainder-concept' (*Restbegriff*) is important. As he insists, we
can never precisely state what the concept of 'nature' is, even
though we may approximate to it by concepts such as that of the
animal rationale. And we can never simply identify the openness
of man's nature to the supernatural by a simple empirical examination of it as we find it, for in it the supernatural may already
be at work, as revelation will subsequently tell us. Substantially
and rather more readably, this point was made as long ago as
1911 by Dom John Chapman is one of his spiritual letters,[86]
but even when those letters were published in 1935 it attracted
little attention. I myself would like to contribute to the discussion the suggestion that, even when we have recognized the
essential fact that, in both the natural and the supernatural order,
the relation between God and man is a relation between personal

[85] See Karl Rahner, *Theological Investigations*, 1, chs. ix, x.

[86] *Spiritual Letters of Dom John Chapman*, Roger Hudleston, ed. (London:
Sheed & Ward, 1935), pp. 192 ff.

beings, we tend to think of this relation in a far too negative way, as if the only manner in which God's activity can come into real contact with man's is by suppressing or at least by diminishing it. The inconclusive and indeed insoluble character of most of the argumentation about the relation between God's primary causality and man's free will, or between divine grace and human freedom seems to me to rest upon this questionable assumption. I will give two examples of this.

My first example, which I have discussed at some length in *The Openness of Being*, is concerned with a very interesting article on the problem of evil by Captain D. H. Doig, in which he writes:

> The act of divine creation must have something paradoxical about it. It cannot confer any benefit on God to create something, because he has the fullness of perfection already. And the first need must be for the Creator to withdraw his universality and omnipotence from a certain sphere in which his creation can operate. . . . Thus to express himself more fully he must surrender some freedom of action. His creation must be a positive act, but since it cannot add to what was already infinite, this must be balanced by a negative withdrawal.[87]

It is the last phrase in this passage that I wish to question.

My other example is from a story which a Jewish rabbi in New York quoted from another rabbi of earlier days in the hearing of Austin Farrer, who reproduced it in one of his sermons:

> The Holy One (Blessed be He!) filled all immensity before the world was, and there was no place where he was not; and so neither was there any place where a world could be; for he was all, and in all. What did he do? He drew back the skirts of his glory, to make a little space

where he was not; and there he created the world. And so, where the
world is, there he is not. And that is why we look in vain for his hand
in the chances of nature. Nevertheless (Blessed be He!) he has visited
us with his loving kindness.

Farrer's comment is as follows:

The world is not like God, though it reveals his power and his glory.
Nature is infinitely wasteful, but God wastes nothing. She is unfeeling;
he is compassionate. She is blind; he is wise. For at the beginning and
bottom of nature, there is a withdrawal, we may almost say a self-
banishment, of God. Nature is not divine; we cannot be nature-
worshippers, except by projecting upon nature a gilded image of our
dreams. God made the world in unlikeness to himself; we look there
in vain for the lineaments of his face. He made man in his own similitude, and it is in the face of man that we must look for the counte-
nance of God.

   Or rather, not in the face of men, but in the faces of men, turned
towards one another. . . . Man's mind, not his bodily frame, is the
similitude of God; and mentality always was a social, not a solitary
thing.[88]

I find both these passages moving and seductive, but, even
when one has allowed for the fact that any language used in this
context is highly analogical, I am very suspicious of any attempt
to account for the secondary causality of creatures by limiting
the primary causality of God. And even Farrer's treatment of
man as a special case does not remove my hesitation. The notion
that God had to withdraw himself from a certain sphere to make
room for his creatures does not seem to me to be a happy one,

[88] A. M. Farrer, *A Celebration of Faith* (London: Hodder & Stoughton,
1972), pp. 72 ff.

and we may notice that in the rabbi's story 'space' is thought of as a kind of receptacle in which God is situated. So far from the creature's existence or its freedom requiring a withdrawal of God from its sphere, I would maintain that both its existence and its freedom are gifts of God and so imply God's entry rather than his withdrawal, though I recognize, of course, that entry, no less than withdrawal, is a highly analogical term.

It seems to me much more satisfactory to start from the traditional position that God moves all secondary causes according to their natures: physical causes according to the nature of physical causes and voluntary causes according to the nature of voluntary causes. For, although this may seem to be a statement of the problem rather than a solution of it, it is, in my view, a statement of the right problem and not of the wrong one. It takes account of two Christian truths: first, that when a man acts in accordance with God's will, God is not excluded from the act or reduced to the condition of a spectator but is the primary agent in it; secondly, that when a man tries to exclude God from the act and make himself the primary agent, all that he manages to do is to introduce an element of sheer destruction and negation, which contravenes his own nature as fundamentally dependent upon God, an element which is not activity but rather deficiency, which goes against his own basic orientation and is therefore self-frustrating and self-destructive. To try to exclude God from one's act is to repudiate one's ontological status as dependent upon God and so to frustrate oneself. In contrast, willingly to invite God as primary cause into one's act is not to abandon or diminish one's own freedom and spontaneity but to augment it. For in relations between persons, in contrast to relations between impersonal mechanical forces, provided the relations are authentically adjusted in accordance with the status and the character of the persons involved, the influence of one does not suppress the freedom and initiative of the other but releases and enhances it. This, which is true of the relations between finite persons, whose activities are in the order of secondary causes, is, I would maintain, not less but more significantly true when one of the causes is the primary causality of the Creator himself. Both on the level of nature and on that of supernature God is to be thought of as bestowing being and not as withholding it. And in saying this, so far from obliterating the distinction between the Creator and the creature, one is emphasizing it. For, the bestowal of being is the essence of creative activity and, as St. Thomas well knew, nobody except God can create.[89]

It has been my chief concern in this lecture to argue that created personal being as such, that is to say, human being, can be elevated into the life of God himself without destruction of its created character. Whether we could have suspected this possibility unless its actuality had been revealed to us, I do not know. I do not think anything precisely like it is claimed by any of the non-Christian religions. What I would claim is that, knowing the fact, we can see at least in retrospect that such a fulfilment is not contrary to the Christian doctrine of creation, as that doctrine applies to the rational creature, man, who bears upon himself the image of God. I would recall the point made by Fr. de Lubac (cited in my first lecture) that human nature and angelic nature are not to be understood simply in the sense in which we speak of animal nature or cosmic nature, that man alone, of all the beings in the world, is capable of beatitude. And here I must mention, however briefly, the central truth of the Christian religion, that God the Son has himself become the hypostatic

[89] *S. Theol.* i, xlv, 5. Much of this and the preceding paragraph is reproduced from *The Openness of Being*, pp. 253 f.

subject of human nature and that this is a far greater wonder and manifests a far nobler possibility in human nature than even the elevation of human persons into the life of God. In St. Thomas's words, 'of all the works of God the mystery of the Incarnation most greatly surpasses our reason; for nothing more wonderful can be thought of that God could do than that very God, the Son of God, should become very man'.[90]

Without trying here to decide whether and in what way grace may be active outside the formal bounds of the visible redeemed community, we may surely say that union with the human nature of the incarnate Son of God is the normal means by which the elevation of men and women into the divine life is brought about, as it also provides the proof that that elevation is possible. To quote St. Thomas again, 'it is no longer incredible that a creature's intellect should be capable of union with God by beholding the divine essence, since the time when God became man by taking human nature to himself'.[91] And the Angelic Doctor is, I think, obviously right in asserting that only a rational nature—one bearing the image of God—could be assumed by a divine Person,[92] and also in asserting that it was most fitting that the Son, rather than the Father or the Holy Spirit, should become incarnate.[93] But I find it difficult to agree with him when he asserts that, less fitting though it would be, an incarnation of the Father or of the Spirit would not be impossible.[94] Rahner's argument that each of the Persons has his special role in the work of man's redemption and that incarnation is the role proper to the Son seems to me to

---

[90] *Contra Gentes*, IV, xxvii.
[91] *Comp. Theol.* I, 201.
[92] *S. Theol.* III, iv, 1.
[93] *Ibid.*, iii, 8.
[94] *Ibid.*, 5.

be convincing.[95] What, however, I am mainly concerned to stress as I come to the end of these lectures is the revelation which the Incarnation gives us of the towering dignity of human nature and of the splendour of the destiny which awaits mankind. For if God himself has assumed human nature, human nature must be the kind of thing that God can assume. In the words of Canon J. A. Baker, 'there must ... be something appropriate about manhood which makes it a possible way of life for God'.[96] I cannot help thinking that, if Pierre Teilhard de Chardin had had a deeper understanding of the historical fact of the Incarnation, it would have given more susbstance to his passionate conviction of the glory of manhood and of creation and would have protected him from some of the charges of unorthodoxy with which he was assailed.

As I conclude, I am as conscious as I am sure my hearers are of the untidy condition in which I have left my subject and of the number of loose ends that need to be tied up. This, however, is perhaps not an entirely surprising or unsatisfactory state of affairs when one is dealing with a living and not a fossilized topic and is professedly contributing to an ongoing discussion. I think it will be clear where my sympathies lie in the turbulent arena of contemporary theological argument. I do not think that the historic beliefs of Christianity are either false or irrelevant to the world in which we live. On the other hand, I think they need both interpretation and development, and that unbalanced and misdirected modes of expression to which they may have become subjected in the course of Christian history need to be corrected.

[95] *The Trinity*, transl. J. Donceel (London: Search Press, and New York: Seabury Press, 1970), pp. 84 f.

[96] *The Foolishness of God* (London: Darton, Longman & Todd, 1970, and New York: Morehouse-Barlow Co., 1971), p. 408.

This is a difficult and delicate task, more difficult and delicate than is recognized by some of its more enthusiastic and self-confident exponents. The thinker who is successful in it will need to be equipped with a large share of the two virtues with which Etienne Gilson has declared that St. Thomas Aquinas was endowed in an uncommonly high degree, namely a perfect intellectual modesty and an almost reckless intellectual audacity.[97] And I am quite sure that, for reasons of strategy no less than of loyalty to the truth, we need to stress the element of transcendence in Christianity. It is largely because the Christian bodies have downgraded transcendence in both teaching and in worship in order to meet what they mistakenly thought to be the needs and demands of man is a secularized age, that men and women, particularly young men and women, have sought to find the transcendence for which they yearn on the purely created and emotional level in the cult of hallucinic drugs and sex, in artificial paradises, because the true paradise has not been offered them. Here if anywhere we see a practical demonstration of the fact that man has by nature a desire for a beatitude that nature itself cannot satisfy, but which God satisfies in grace by the free and unconditioned gift of himself.

[97] *Reason and Revelation in the Middle Ages* (New York: Charles Scribner's Sons, 1938), p. 71.

LECTURE THREE: DISCUSSION

Question 1:

It would seem from your definition of nature and supernature that one might be able to infer that you would think that the proof for the immortality of the soul is not natural since it does not deal with 'this life' and 'this world'.

Mascall:

I don't think that the immortality of the soul can be *conclusively* proved by purely natural arguments. In holding that view I am in agreement with at least some of the medieval thinkers. St. Thomas did hold that one could by reason prove the immortality of the soul, in the sense that unless God deliberately decided to destroy it, the soul had a natural immortality. But I am prepared to leave the question open.

Question 2:

In Aquinas' understanding, man is in a relationship of intelligible causal dependence on God whereas God is not causally dependent on man. It is in the context of causal dependence that Aquinas stated that man is really related to God whereas God is only notionally related to man. Do you think that there is a tendency today to confuse the language of metaphysics with the language of personalism, and that modern objections to Aquinas' position may be the result of such a confusion?

Mascall:

I never thought about the matter just in this way. There is a problem of reconciling the immutability of God, the unchangingness of God, with God's changing concern with the world, of reconciling his impassibility with his compassion, and it seems to me that this suggestion is one which would be in fact very much worthwhile following out. I would not want to go into this question right now.

Question 3:

In your lecture you seem to be in agreement with Rahner that we cannot know *precisely* what human nature is like. Do you mean by this that it is never possible for us to determine exactly and precisely whether a certain quality in man, *e.g.*, his rationality, is natural or supernatural?

Mascall:

I think we can recognize certain human qualities as being natural and I think rationality is one of them. If man were only a creature of this world, only concerned with living this life, he would need certain qualities to do this. But I think that just because we only know him as graced by God, or at least because we are never sure that any particular person is not graced by God, it is not possible by empirical investigation precisely to determine which things in human beings come from nature and which from grace.

But it seems to me that by and large we get a pretty clear notion of what it is in man that is concerned simply with his life in this world, and what in fact is concerned with the beatific vision. Man's nature is open to the supernatural as such, not closed. It does not seem to me that from a practical point of view this is a very serious problem.

Question 4:

With respect to the natural desire to see God, would you care to comment on this remark of Bernard Lonergan: 'The desire and its fulfilment must have the same material object. But a desire to understand cannot have the same formal object as the fulfilling act of understanding. A desire to understand is specified by what we already know. The fulfilling act is specified by what as yet we do not know. Thus, the object of the natural desire is transcendental [that is to say, I believe, it is the object of the pure desire to know, or the notion of being, that *Insight* speaks of]; but the object of the fulfilling vision is supernatural.'[1]

Mascall:

I have not had the opportunity of looking at the context in which this citation occurs. Lonergan seems to be suggesting that the natural desire, the desire of transcending the natural, is not ex-

[1] 'The Natural Desire to See God', in *Collection*, ed. F. E. Crowe, S.J. (London: Darton, Longman & Todd, and New York: Herder and Herder, 1967), p. 90.

plicitly a desire for the creator of that desire, but nevertheless, if this desire is to be fulfilled, only the creator can fulfill it. If that is what he means—and I am not sure it is—I think I have difficulty with the assertion that the object of the natural desire is merely something beyond this life and this world.

In later writings Lonergan takes up the Thomist tag that nothing can be desired, nothing can be loved, unless it is already known. He asserts that particular principle does not apply when it is a question of the desire for God. I think it is clear that Lonergan's recognition of that particular general principle (Nothing can be desired and loved unless it is previously known) does not preclude his asserting that that principle does not apply to our loving God. God, and God alone, can be loved before he is known. I think only recently Lonergan has come to state that position. But I would like to check dates and context, and things like that. I would personally hold that there is a natural desire, not merely for something that transcends this world and this life, but a desire to see the creator.

Question 5:

Could you elaborate on what you consider to be the correct understanding of the difference between created and uncreated grace? Do you think that the West has perhaps underemphasized the insight that is at the roots of the Eastern stress on uncreated grace?

Mascall:

Certainly the pure nature view, which was held in the West for a good long time, is vulnerable to the criticism which the Easterns have made. But I think that if grace is something that relates man to God and God to man, it must have both an uncreated and a created aspect. And according to what I consider the correct understanding of the difference between created and uncreated grace, the difference between the two is simply the difference between looking at the same thing from two opposite poles. Any relation between God and man is a very mysterious thing. It is obvious that a God who is absolutely perfect can create creatures, but any relation between God and man is bound to have a created and uncreated aspect. I find the Easterns rather perverse in their insistence that grace is simply uncreated. It seems to me that if you take that attitude, then you would tend to be saying that grace simply turns man into the uncreated God. I believe that grace does allow the lifting up of man into the life of God with the proviso that this does not in fact destroy man's complete dependence upon God but rather enhances it.

Question 6:

Although you say in your lecture that you have not the intention 'to discuss systematically the various nuances which the notion of grace has acquired in the course of Christian history', would it not be fair to ask if you have not actually discussed grace essentially in terms that presuppose the distinction of created and uncreated grace, especially if one takes into account your definition of grace?

Mascall:

I think I would answer Yes. All that I meant was that I was not going to attempt in this lecture to discuss one by one all these

distinctions about grace. But I think in fact the question of created grace and uncreated grace is quite essential to our discussion.
I wanted to protect myself from the objection that I had discussed grace without making any distinctions. One simply can't
do everything in one lecture.

Question 7:

On the distinction natural and supernatural: you mentioned
many times that we can at least point to the fact that man seems
to live for certain things: at certain times concerned about this
world, at other times with the other world. I was wondering
about the insight of certain Christian mystics, that one's ordinary
actions of the day are not divorced from the supernatural end.
At the end of your lecture, when discussing freedom, you said
that an attempt to cut off God would frustrate the natural aspect
of man. My question: is there any critical value then in making
this distinction between the natural and supernatural in man,
or perhaps more value in the merging of these, like in the view
of the Christian mystics?

Mascall:

I think it is really important. I intended among other things to
stress the importance of man's concern with the things of this
world and the fact that this in fact depends on the relation between
grace and nature. Even man's natural activities are directed towards the beatific vision. Anything conducive to that beatific
vision is such because grace elevates nature, not destroys it. And
I do not think that Christian mystics in any way pretend to suggest that because of their concern with God, because of their

having been given a kind of anticipation of the beatific vision, of heaven, they are tempted to consider their worldly duties as a nuisance. It is the other way around, I think, Christian belief is that this world is not merely something which man passes through but something to be transformed at the last day. So I would not suggest religion is only concerned with religious things, and not concerned with the ordinary needs of life, like some forms of Eastern religions. Since they do not recognize the relation of nature and grace, they can in effect appear very unconcerned with the problems, sufferings, joys, and what not, of the ordinary life of human beings.

Question 8:

What would be your response to the neo-orthodox view of Barth on the relation of grace and nature?

Mascall:

I think that Barth, as Pius XII said, may well be perhaps the greatest theologian of the century. But there is an assumption in Barth that I was attacking, that there is some opposition between God and man, or between grace and nature, or between grace and human freedom. This I deny. Even aside from man's alienation by sin, and speaking of man simply as created by God—it seems to me that the Barthian man is radically opposed to God.

Man is in fact just the opposite. Man is created by God in God's image. I think that one of the most unfortunate things in some Protestant theologians, in Tillich as well as in Barth, is a tendency to confuse the fall with creation, to think that man is in opposition to God simply because he is a creature and not because he has fallen into a condition of sin. But it does seem to me that to take man's fallen condition, which is in the strict sense accidental, as if it were the basic thing in man's relation to God, is very mistaken.

Question 9:

It seems to me that in our explanation of sin and man's ability to sin, frequently we use the metaphor that God creates free will and thus ties his own hands. I was wondering if you could pursue that to explore the possibilities of explaining a deeper understanding of what freedom really means in this context.

Mascall:

I would come back to my assertion that God in creating is not in fact withdrawing himself but is communicating himself. There is a question of how God does communicate himself to a creature. But something like that must be the case if creation is possible at all. So it seems to me that God in giving man freedom is not withdrawing himself, but rather he is communicating himself in a particular way.

It seems to me that the fact that man's freedom can sometimes at least appear to be a kind of contradiction of God's own supremacy is due to the fact that freedom is in fact *received*. There is of course a question of how it is possible for man to do something contrary to the will of the creator. However, it is not a question of excluding God from a certain sphere; the question arises not because God has withdrawn himself, but because God has given himself to man.

But if man is authentically free, he is in fact acting as a kind of an extension of God's activity, and not as a limit upon him. One should start off by thinking that freedom is a gift by God to man by which God intends to make man more receptive of him, more closely united with God. God does not set man up as an opponent. There are no beings which have a sphere in which he is not acting.